TEACHER GUIDE FOR
SUGAR FALLS

Learning About the History and Legacy of Residential Schools in Grades 9–12

Christine M'Lot

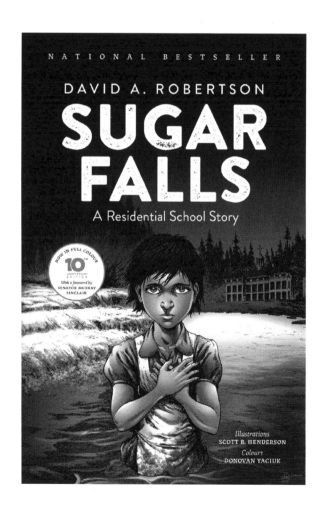

PORTAGE & MAIN PRESS

Portage & Main Press gratefully acknowledges the financial support of the Province of Manitoba through the Department of Sport, Culture and Heritage and the Manitoba Book Publishing Tax Credit, and the Government of Canada through the Canada Book Fund (CBF) for our publishing activities.

Printed and bound in Canada by Prolific Group
Design by Jennifer Lum

Thank you to David A. Robertson, Scott B. Henderson, Donovan Yaciuk, and Betty Ross for making this important history accessible for young people.
—CM

Also issued in electronic format: ISBN 978-1-77492-009-1 (PDF)

24 23 22 21   1 2 3 4 5

PORTAGE &
MAIN PRESS
www.portageandmainpress.com
Winnipeg, Manitoba
Treaty 1 Territory and homeland of the Métis Nation

CONTENTS

USING THIS GUIDE

THIS GUIDE SUPPORTS teachers of *Sugar Falls: A Residential School Story* (10th anniversary edition) in creating dynamic learning experiences for their students, while maintaining a respectful and dignified approach to Indigenous topics. This guide is divided into three main parts: Part 1: Before Reading *Sugar Falls*; Part 2: While Reading *Sugar Falls*; and Part 3: After Reading *Sugar Falls*. These are followed by resources for students and teachers that support the activities suggested here and will deepen students' understanding of residential schools in Canada.

Part 1: Before Reading *Sugar Falls* (page 13) consists of activities that serve to enhance prior knowledge about the topics addressed in *Sugar Falls* and to prepare students for sensitive topics in a way that is consistent with a trauma-informed practice (see next section of this introduction).

Part 2: While Reading *Sugar Falls* (page 45) provides activities to do while reading *Sugar Falls*.

Part 3: After Reading *Sugar Falls* (page 69) includes culminating activities to do after students have finished reading *Sugar Falls*. You are not meant to do every activity; rather, this guide offers a menu of suggested activities to choose from based on the needs and interests of your students. There are activities that fit well for whole-class instruction and discussion as well as activities for individuals or small groups. Part 1 also includes two suggestions for whole-school activities. Each activity indicates the amount of class time required to complete it. Please note that this does not include time spent outside class on reading, research, or other homework.

Sugar Falls: A Residential School Story includes sensitive topics (e.g., abuse, trauma); therefore, it is most appropriate for grades 9–12. The activities in this guide are most appropriate for courses such as English Language Arts, Social Studies, History, Global or Contemporary Issues, as well as Current Topics in First Nations, Métis, and Inuit Studies. They could be adapted for use at the university or college level. A number of these activities encourage cross-curricular connections (e.g., arts education, psychology, physical education/health education, mathematics, science) and collaborations with other teachers.

TEACHER GUIDE FOR SUGAR FALLS: A RESIDENTIAL SCHOOL STORY © 2021 PORTAGE & MAIN PRESS ISBN:978-1-77492-010-7

Many activities incorporate Indigenous pedagogical practice by having students work collaboratively. Other activities have students take on the role of expert and teacher, often through student-led research. Working in relation with others, seeking holism in understanding, and learning through storytelling are key practices in Indigenous pedagogy. This teacher guide aims to serve as a tool for engaging students in the complexity of understanding and embracing worldviews that may be different from their own.

Please see Resources for Teachers at the end of this guide (page 95) for helpful resources related to Indigenous pedagogy.

WHAT IS TRAUMA-INFORMED PRACTICE?

Trauma-informed practice means consciously working "to understand how violence, victimization, and other traumatic experiences may have figured in the lives of the individuals involved and to apply that understanding to the provision of services and the design of systems so that they accommodate the needs and vulnerabilities of trauma survivors."[1] Although originally designed as a framework for delivering social services, trauma-informed practice can be relevant to educational settings when students are learning about topics that could traumatize (or retraumatize) them. The goal of trauma-informed practice is to decrease the likelihood of traumatizing students through exposing them to traumatic narratives—such as the residential school story in *Sugar Falls*.

TEACHING DIFFICULT TOPICS FROM A TRAUMA-INFORMED STANCE

As is often true when learning about Indigenous subjects, sensitive topics may come up when your students are reading, researching, or learning about *Sugar Falls*. The story told through this graphic novel describes traumatic experiences such as suicide, violence, physical abuse, and sexual abuse. Even more heartbreaking is the realization that these things did happen, happened frequently, and happened to young children.

If you have Indigenous students in your class, it is very likely that someone in their family attended residential school; however, never assume that these students have access to their family's histories or that what happened at residential school has been shared with them. A

---

[1] Lisa D. Butler, Filomena M. Critelli, and Elaine S. Rinfrette, "Trauma-Informed Care and Mental Health," *Directions in Psychiatry* 31, no. 3 (January 2011): 197–208, <https://www.researchgate.net/publication/234155324_Trauma-Informed_Care_and_Mental_Health.>

trauma-informed practice uses the utmost caution and care while teaching about the history and legacy of residential schools. A medicine wheel goal-setting activity has been included in this guide to help students set mental health goals and process their emotions while reading *Sugar Falls*.

Teaching about residential schools from a trauma-informed stance means placing a high emphasis on informing students about resources that are available to them if they should feel overwhelmed or triggered at any point. Throughout the process of preparing to read, reading, and responding to this story, create a safe and open learning environment where students' mental health is supported. Often, direct discussions about mental health and wellness are great ways for students to hear from others and learn positive coping skills to help them in their learning journeys. Helpful information and advice for teachers on how to build flourishing learning communities and address mental-health needs with all students can be found in *Ensouling Our Schools: A Universally Designed Framework for Mental Health, Well-Being, and Reconciliation* by Jennifer Katz with Kevin Lamoureux.

Finally, while reading this graphic novel with your class, include positive aspects of Indigenous histories and cultures to show the beauty and resilience in our communities. Suggested in this resource are ways to bring Indigenous cultures, languages, traditions, and beliefs into your classroom; these include inviting an Elder or Knowledge Keeper to speak to your students about a positive aspect of Indigenous culture (see activities in parts 2 and 3 of this guide). Keep in mind that Indigenous Nations are distinct and each have their own cultures, languages, ceremonies, stories, and traditions. Learning about Indigenous culture can be a strong protective factor for Indigenous students while learning about difficult topics.

THE HISTORY AND LEGACY OF RESIDENTIAL SCHOOLS

It would be impossible to overstate the significance of the history and legacy of residential schools in Canada. Between 1867 and 1996, at least 150 000 children were taken from their homes and sent to government-funded, church-run schools.[2] Below are some key points in history that teachers are encouraged to explore further.

- John A. Macdonald, Canada's founding prime minister, is regarded as the architect of the residential school system and for this reason is a controversial figure in Canadian history.[3] While many Canadians—past and present—believe that the sole purpose of these schools

---

[2] "The Residential School System," Parks Canada, Government of Canada, 1 September 2020, <https://www.canada.ca/en/parks-canada/news/2020/09/the-residential-school-system.html#shr-pg0>.

[3] Sean Carleton, "John A. Macdonald Was the Real Architect of Residential Schools," *Toronto Star*, 9 July 2017, <https://www.thestar.com/opinion/commentary/2017/07/09/john-a-macdonald-was-the-real-architect-of-residential-schools.html>.

was to educate Indigenous children and help them integrate into settler society, the result was catastrophic and continues to negatively affect Indigenous people to this day. Through the residential school system, the government alienated children from their families, culture, language, spirituality, and land, and ultimately caused the breakdown of the family unit.

- The history of interactions between Indigenous peoples and what would become Canada is complicated. Indigenous Nations helped the French and British settlers navigate the terrain and showed them how to survive during the harsh winter months.[4] Many Indigenous Nations had lucrative trade deals with the French and British.[5] Some Indigenous Nations, such as the Shawnee, even fought alongside the British against the United States in the War of 1812, leading to the defeat of US expansion into Canada.[6] Although British and Canadian allyship with Indigenous Nations cannot be overlooked, the British broke many of the promises that they made to Indigenous Nations.

- The 1867 Indian Act came to define life for Indigenous peoples for over a hundred years, and arguably continues to do so to this day. Through the Indian Act—a race-based legislation—Indigenous people could not vote, run for office, hire lawyers, or even use farming equipment. The Indian Act also paved the way for the residential school system.

- While education was important to Indigenous people, and leaders advocated for education to be included in treaties, Indigenous families did not have a choice in sending their children to residential schools. They were often threatened with jail time if they hesitated to send their children.

- Today, we continue to see the effects of residential schools, which produced generations of Indigenous people who struggle with identity, cultural pride, and community.

---

[4] P. Whitney Lackenbauer, John Moses, R. Scott Sheffield, Maxime Gohier, *Aboriginal People in the Canadian Military* (Department of National Defense, 2018), chap. 1, <https://www.canada.ca/en/department-national-defence/services/military-history/history-heritage/popular-books/aboriginal-people-canadian-military/arrival-europeans-17th-century-wars.html>.

[5] "First Nations in Canada." Crown-Indigenous Relations and Northern Affairs Canada, Government of Canada, 2 May 2017, <https://www.rcaanc-cirnac.gc.ca/eng/1307460755710/1536862806124>.

[6] James Miller, updated by Zach Parrott, "Indigenous-British Relations Pre-Confederation," *Canadian Encyclopedia*, 26 May 2015, <https://www.thecanadianencyclopedia.ca/en/article/aboriginal-european-relations>.

TEACHING GRAPHIC NOVELS

The terms *graphic novel* and *comic book* describe the format of a book, rather than a genre. Graphic novels and comic books can be fiction, nonfiction, biography, fantasy, dystopia, or any genre in between.[7] Graphic novels are an accessible reading resource for all students, and they have been proven to engage even the most reluctant of readers.[8] Graphic novels include many elements (e.g., dialogue, characters' thoughts, narration, captions) and are meant to be read from left to right and top to bottom. For more information and ideas for using graphic novels in the classroom, see *Teaching With Graphic Novels* by Shelley Stagg Peterson, available through Portage & Main Press, and the student resource *How Comics Work* by Candida Rifkind and Brandon Christopher (illustrated by Alice RL), published online by the Department of English at the University of Winnipeg, at <https://www.uwinnipeg.ca/1b19/docs/how-comics-work-web-cc-by-nc-nd.pdf>.

INVITING AN ELDER INTO YOUR LEARNING SPACE

Teachers may want to engage the larger community and invite an Elder or Knowledge Keeper to share stories, knowledge, or teachings with the class. This can be a great way to highlight positive aspects of Indigenous histories and cultures. If you ask an Elder or Knowledge Keeper to share their own stories about attending residential school and their journey to healing, be aware that you are asking people to speak about their trauma. This is a conversation that should be had with great care and sensitivity.

Here are some guidelines on building a positive relationship with a local Elder or Knowledge Keeper. The *Western Canadian Protocol Framework for Aboriginal Language and Culture Programs* defines an Elder as "any person regarded or chosen by an Aboriginal Nation to be the keeper and teacher of its oral tradition and knowledge," but it is important to remember that this definition may vary from community to community.[9]

---

[7] "What is a Graphic Novel?" Get Graphic, Buffalo and Erie County Public Library and partnering organizations, accessed, <https://www.buffalolib.org/get-graphic/what-graphic-novel>.

[8] Sarah Knutson, "How Graphic Novels Help Students Develop Critical Skills," Resilient Educator, accessed 20 July 2021, <https://resilienteducator.com/classroom-resources/graphic-novels-visual-literacy/>.

[9] Quoted in Manitoba Education and Youth, *Integrating Aboriginal Perspectives Into Curricula* (Government of Manitoba, 2003), 12, <https://www.edu.gov.mb.ca/k12/docs/policy/abpersp/ab_persp.pdf>.

TEACHER GUIDE FOR SUGAR FALLS: A RESIDENTIAL SCHOOL STORY © 2021 PORTAGE & MAIN PRESS ISBN: 978-1-77492-010-7

BEFORE THE MEETING

- Ask your school board or Indigenous Education lead if they have an Elder-in-residence or a trusted Elder or Knowledge Keeper whom they regularly ask to speak with students.

- Research the protocols in your community (e.g., passing tobacco) for inviting an Elder to speak with your class. If you are unsure about the protocols, ask the Elder what would be appropriate.

- Arrange a meeting to speak with the Elder well in advance of their planned visit to your class.

PLANNING THE VISIT

- Share a bit about yourself and your family's history.

- Listen and learn from the Elder.

- Adhere to the protocols in your area and ask the Elder if they would be interested in sharing their gifts with your class.

- Be as flexible about the day and time for the visit as you can. Decide this together!

- Ask if the Elder needs any special accommodations for when they come.

- Discuss fair compensation. The Elder may be taking the day off work to accommodate your needs, so make sure they are well compensated for their time, energy, and emotional labour.

- Ask the Elder if they would prefer to receive a list of students' questions beforehand so they can plan their answers and only answer the questions they are comfortable answering. This may be especially true if they are being asked about their experiences at residential school.

THE DAY OF THE VISIT

- Welcome the Elder to your class/school. Have a student volunteer present the Elder with the tobacco tie (depending on the protocol in your region).

- Give the Elder a tour of your school, if possible. At the very least, make sure they know where the washrooms are if needed.

- Ask the Elder how they would like to be introduced to your class.

- Ensure students are respectful while the Elder is speaking.

- Thank the Elder at the end and present them with their honorarium.

It is recommended that you build a relationship with a local Elder or Knowledge Keeper. Relationships take time to develop, so you should contact the Elder as soon as possible. If the day goes well, be sure to let them know that you will be inviting them back!

TEACHER GUIDE FOR SUGAR FALLS: A RESIDENTIAL SCHOOL STORY © 2021 PORTAGE & MAIN PRESS ISBN: 978-1-77492-010-7

BEFORE READING
SUGAR FALLS

The following activities will prepare students to engage with the topics presented in *Sugar Falls* and prepare them for sensitive topics in a way that is consistent with a trauma-informed practice. When deciding which activities are appropriate for your students, consider subject area connections and students' individual learning interests.

Activities for the Classroom (page 13) are suitable for small-group or whole-class instruction, while Whole-School Activities (page 37) include ideas to get the whole student body involved in commemorating Orange Shirt Day or creating a Living Library.

TEACHER GUIDE FOR SUGAR FALLS: A RESIDENTIAL SCHOOL STORY © 2021 PORTAGE & MAIN PRESS ISBN: 978-1-77492-010-7

TEACHER GUIDE FOR SUGAR FALLS: A RESIDENTIAL SCHOOL STORY © 2021 PORTAGE & MAIN PRESS   ISBN: 978-1-77492-010-7

ACTIVITIES FOR THE CLASSROOM

- What Is Wellness From an Indigenous Perspective?

- Learn the History

- Analyze Children's Art

- Research Ethics and Experiments Conducted on Children in Residential Schools

TEACHER GUIDE FOR SUGAR FALLS: A RESIDENTIAL SCHOOL STORY © 2021 PORTAGE & MAIN PRESS ISBN: 978-1-77492-010-7

WHAT IS WELLNESS FROM AN INDIGENOUS PERSPECTIVE?

TEACHER GUIDE FOR SUGAR FALLS: A RESIDENTIAL SCHOOL STORY © 2021 PORTAGE & MAIN PRESS ISBN: 978-1-77492-010-7

SUBJECT AREA CONNECTIONS

Social Studies / English Language Arts / Physical Education / Health Education

GOALS OF THESE ACTIVITIES

Students will learn about Indigenous perspectives on wellness relating to all parts of the self—physical, spiritual, mental, and emotional—and set goals in each category to facilitate holism, balance, and wellness in their lives. Students will learn the value of self-care and why it is especially important while learning about difficult topics, such as those presented in *Sugar Falls*.

BEFORE YOU BEGIN

- Review "The Seven Lessons of the Medicine Wheel," by Kelly J. Beaulieu, at <https://saymag.com/the-seven-lessons-of-the-medicine-wheel/>, and the video "Medicine Wheel Goal Setting" (15:36), on my YouTube channel, *Christine M'Lot*, at <https://www.youtube.com/watch?v=0N9bI9FSbcA>.

- Familiarize yourself with the mental health supports available to students in your school and community. Consider inviting a school counsellor to speak to your students about mental health and healthy coping skills (see Steps to Follow) or an Elder or Knowledge Keeper to speak to your students about wellness from an Indigenous perspective (see Inviting an Elder Into Your Learning Space on page 9 of this guide).

- Review the concept of SMART goals. See, for instance, "An Interactive Lesson Plan for Teaching Students How to Set S.M.A.R.T. Goals," at <https://www.teachervision.com/blog/morning-announcements/an-interactive-lesson-plan-for-teaching-students-how-to-set-smart-goals>.

Set Wellness Goals Using the Medicine Wheel

TEACHER GUIDE FOR SUGAR FALLS: A RESIDENTIAL SCHOOL STORY © 2021 PORTAGE & MAIN PRESS ISBN: 978-1-77492-010-7

DURATION

1 hour

OVERVIEW

Schools often don't explicitly teach students how to be *well*. Throughout this lesson, students will learn about the Anishinaabe perspective on wellness, which relates to all parts of the self: physical, spiritual, mental, and emotional. Students will set goals in each category to facilitate holism, balance, and wellness in their lives. Students will also learn the value of self-care and why it is especially important while learning about difficult topics, such as those presented in *Sugar Falls*.

STEPS TO FOLLOW

• Inform the class that today's lesson will be centred on the concept of wellness. Wellness as defined from an Anishinaabe perspective is when all the parts of ourselves—physical, spiritual, mental, and emotional—are in balance.

• Have the class brainstorm answers to the question "What does it mean to be 'well'?" Write students' answers on the whiteboard or on chart paper, so students have a visual prompt as to what wellness might look and feel like. Inform students that wellness looks and feels different to different people, and that it is important for us to know what wellness looks and feels like for us personally.

• Draw a circle on the whiteboard and divide it into four quadrants. Label them "Physical," "Spiritual," "Mental," and "Emotional." Explain to students that this is a medicine wheel.

• Have students take out a piece of blank paper and draw a large medicine wheel. Next, have them divide the wheel into four quadrants, and label the quadrants "Physical," "Spiritual," "Mental," and "Emotional," as shown on the whiteboard. Explain to students that if giving a teaching, an Elder or Knowledge Keeper would explain which quadrant represents which part of the self, but for this activity the order of the labels is unimportant.

TEACHER GUIDE FOR SUGAR FALLS: A RESIDENTIAL SCHOOL STORY © 2021 PORTAGE & MAIN PRESS   ISBN: 978-1-77492-010-7

- Explain that the four quadrants can represent many things, such as the four directions, the four phases of life, or the four sacred medicines. Then explain to students that they will use the medicine wheel to examine and think about the four parts of the self—physical, spiritual, mental, and emotional—and how it is important for the parts to be balanced if we truly want to be well. Advise students that we are also doing this activity to ensure that we can look after ourselves while learning about difficult topics, such as those presented in *Sugar Falls*.

- Provide students with information regarding the mental health supports that are available to them in the school and community. For example, invite a school counsellor to teach students about mental health and healthy coping skills. Create a list of healthy coping skills as a class, so students can choose the skills they are most likely to use to set goals.

- Have students set goals for themselves that fit each quadrant and write the goals on scrap paper. Explain that some goals may fit in two or more quadrants, but they should pick the category that makes the most sense for them. It may be helpful to give some examples of goals for each quadrant:

  > physical goals (health, fitness): I will lift weights once per week.

  > spiritual goals (religious practice, focusing on self, family, community, or anything that makes our "spirit" happy): I will practise my culture with my family once a month.

  > mental goals (knowledge, school): I want to learn about outer space.

  > emotional (mental health): I will practise deep breathing when I feel stressed.

- Students should set at least three goals for each of the four quadrants.

- Then have students transform their goals into SMART goals. SMART stands for Specific, Measurable, Attainable, Realistic, and Time-bound. Model how to create a SMART goal for students, such as in the following example:

Original Goals	SMART Goals
I will eat healthily.	• I will eat three servings of vegetables every day. • I will limit myself to one sugary snack a day.

- Have students add their SMART goals in the appropriate quadrants of their medicine wheels. This really gets them thinking!

- Finally, have students colour the four quadrants using the traditional colours black, yellow, white, and red (for example, physical = black, spiritual = yellow, mental = white, emotional = red). Again, if an Elder or Knowledge Keeper were giving a teaching, they would explain the colours and what they represent.

ASSESSMENT

Since this assignment is highly personal, it is often difficult to grade.

Summative: Assess for completeness (e.g., does the student have at least three goals for each quadrant?) and for evidence of understanding of SMART goals in the way the goals are written.

TEACHER GUIDE FOR SUGAR FALLS: A RESIDENTIAL SCHOOL STORY © 2021 PORTAGE & MAIN PRESS ISBN: 978-1-77492-010-7

Assess Wellness Using the Medicine Wheel

TEACHER GUIDE FOR SUGAR FALLS: A RESIDENTIAL SCHOOL STORY © 2021 PORTAGE & MAIN PRESS   ISBN: 978-1-77492-010-7

DURATION

0.5 hours

OVERVIEW

As a follow-up to the previous activity, students will use the medicine wheel to self-assess wellness.

STEPS TO FOLLOW

- Model the check-in with students by drawing a large medicine wheel on the whiteboard. Label the quadrants with the four parts of the self: physical, spiritual, mental, and emotional.

- Explain to students that you are going to rate your own feelings of wellness today using the four categories. Draw a dot where you feel your own level of wellness is today. Dots near the centre of the circle indicate you are not doing too well in that category; dots near the outer edge indicate you feel well.

- Connect your dots to form a circle shape. Circles that look like the medicine wheel indicate you are feeling well and balanced in all areas, whereas small circles or other shapes indicate you need to work on some areas today. A small circle near the centre would indicate a general feeling of unwellness. Sometimes, if we are feeling unbalanced in one area, it can make us feel unwell without knowing why. This activity should highlight areas in which students are feeling well or unwell so they (possibly together with their teacher) can then self-assess the behaviours that could help them re-balance to increase feelings of overall wellness. See the illustration for an example.

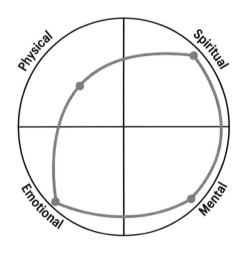

- **How I'm feeling today**

- Meet one-on-one with each student to discuss their wellness levels and have a conversation about how they can increase their wellness in areas that they rated lower. For example, if a student gives their physical wellness a low rating, discuss why that is and what they could do to improve their wellness for tomorrow. If they often feel tired, they may want to work on going to bed earlier.

ASSESSMENT

Formative: Use the medicine wheel as a tool to check in on students' wellness throughout the year in teacher-student interviews.

TEACHER GUIDE FOR SUGAR FALLS: A RESIDENTIAL SCHOOL STORY © 2021 PORTAGE & MAIN PRESS   ISBN: 978-1-77492-010-7

LEARN THE HISTORY

TEACHER GUIDE FOR SUGAR FALLS: A RESIDENTIAL SCHOOL STORY © 2021 PORTAGE & MAIN PRESS ISBN: 978-1-77492-010-7

SUBJECT AREA CONNECTIONS

Social Studies / English Language Arts

GOAL OF THESE ACTIVITIES

One of the simplest ways to begin learning about Indigenous topics is to learn about the Indigenous Nations whose traditional territory the school is on. Through these mini-research activities, students will learn the history of the land they live and learn on. Students can choose to do this activity based on where they go to school or where their home is, if home is in a different area.

What Indigenous Territory Are We On?

DURATION

1 hour

OVERVIEW

Students will conduct individual, paired, or small-group research to identify which traditional territory (or territories) their school or home is on.

BEFORE YOU BEGIN

Students may have studied the history of residential schools more than once in earlier grades. Depending on where your classroom is located and the background of your students, consider reviewing this history with the class. See The History and Legacy of Residential Schools in the introduction to this guide (page 7) and Resources for Teachers (page 88).

STEPS TO FOLLOW

- Ask students if they know the Indigenous territory they are on. Introduce students to one of the following resources, as appropriate:

    > BC: Indigenous Foundations, at <https://indigenousfoundations.arts.ubc.ca/home/>

    > Manitoba: "Map of the Numbered Treaties," at <http://www.trcm.ca/treaties/treaties-in-manitoba/view-pdf-interactive-map-of-numbered-treaties-trcm-july-20-entry/>

    > Ontario: "Ontario First Nations Maps" at <https://www.ontario.ca/page/ontario-first-nations-maps#section-0>

    > Other provinces, territories, and countries: Native Land, at <https://native-land.ca>

    Note: According to its creators, Native Land's map is a work in progress and does not represent or intend to represent official or legal boundaries of any Indigenous Nations. To learn about definitive boundaries, contact the Nations in question.

TEACHER GUIDE FOR SUGAR FALLS: A RESIDENTIAL SCHOOL STORY © 2021 PORTAGE & MAIN PRESS ISBN: 978-1-77492-010-7

- Then give students the following questions to research, either individually, in pairs, or in small groups:

    1. Which Indigenous Nations lived in this area before colonization?
    2. What languages did they speak?
    3. What did they call this territory?
    4. Which Nations live here now?
    5. Were treaties signed? If so, which ones?
        > Who signed the treaties?
        > What is written in these treaties?
        > Were the treaties honoured?

- Consider assigning different questions to different groups and having groups teach what they have learned to the rest of the class. If students are comfortable with the jigsaw method of organizing group work, that would be effective here. (For more information, see The Jigsaw Classroom, at <https://www.jigsaw.org>.)

- Have students follow up with a written reflection in which they assess what they have learned from this activity and what they would like to know next.

ASSESSMENT

Summative: Have students assess their own and other groups' presentations for completeness and clarity: did they answer the assigned questions and explain their answers in a helpful way?

Formative: Review written reflections to assess students' readiness for reading *Sugar Falls*; plan supports and encouragements accordingly.

TEACHER GUIDE FOR SUGAR FALLS: A RESIDENTIAL SCHOOL STORY © 2021 PORTAGE & MAIN PRESS   ISBN: 978-1-77492-010-7

Where Were the Residential Schools in Our Area, and What Was Their Purpose?

DURATION

1 hour

OVERVIEW

Students will conduct research about the residential school(s) that were in their local area and explore the purpose of the schools.

STEPS TO FOLLOW

- Assess students' prior knowledge about residential schools by having them complete a KWL Chart. Have students make their own chart by folding a piece of paper into three columns and labeling them as follows:

What I Know	What I Want to Know	What I Learned

- In the first column, have students write everything they already know about residential schools. In the second column, have students write everything they want to know about residential schools. Leave the last column blank for now.

- Individually, in pairs, or in small groups, have students use CBC's interactive map "Did You Live Near a Residential School?," at <https://www.cbc.ca/ncws2/intcractivcs/beyond-94-residential-school-map/>, to locate the residential school that was either nearest to where they live or nearest to where they now to go school. Give students the option of using their home addresses or the address of the school to find the nearest residential school.

TEACHER GUIDE FOR SUGAR FALLS: A RESIDENTIAL SCHOOL STORY © 2021 PORTAGE & MAIN PRESS   ISBN: 978-1-77492-010-7

- Have students write down what they learn about the following information in the "What I Learned" section of the KWL Chart:

    1. What was the name of the school?
    2. How far away from you was it?
    3. What were its years of operation?

    Note: "Did You Live Near a Residential School?" does not provide the years of operation for every school. Reassure students that if they cannot find that information here, they will be able to find it in the next research step.

- Give students time to compare their answers and discuss their reactions to what they have learned. (Were they surprised? Had they ever heard of this school before?)

- Now that students have identified particular schools, have them do further online research to see what other facts they can find about these schools from the National Centre for Truth and Reconciliation (NCTR) Archives, at <https://archives.nctr.ca/actor/browse?sort=alphabetiC&SortDir=asC&EntityType=840>. Explain to them that the following kinds of information can help them understand the purpose of residential schools. They are not expected to answer every question or investigate in depth; they are just asked to see what else they can learn with a little research.

    1. Who ran the school (the Catholic Church? the Presbyterian Church? another Protestant church?)?
    2. How many students did the school house at any given time, of what ages?
    3. Where were these students' homes?
    4. What was taught there? Which curriculum, and which grades?
    5. What rules did students have to follow?

    Note: The NCTR Archives contain primary source materials. Students may require teacher assistance.

- Have students write down additional facts they have learned in the "What I Learned" section of the KWL chart.

- Give students time to compare their answers and discuss what they have learned. How would they describe the purpose of the school they researched? (For instance, they might say that the purpose of a school was to teach western religion and culture, or they might say that the purpose of a school was to separate children from their homes.)

- Based on their answers in the KWL chart, if students are interested in learning more about the purpose of residential schools, encourage them to explore the following resources and add what they learn to the "What I Learned" section of the KWL chart:

> "Heritage Minutes: Chanie Wenjack" (1:00), at <https://www.historicacanada.ca/content/heritage-minutes/chanie-wenjack>

> *Residential Schools in Canada: History and Legacy Education Guide*, at <http://www.education.historicacanada.ca/en/tools/647>

ASSESSMENT

Formative: Assess for evidence of understanding by observing and supporting students as they work.

Summative: Have students hand in their completed KWL charts. Assess students' charts for completeness and accuracy.

TEACHER GUIDE FOR SUGAR FALLS: A RESIDENTIAL SCHOOL STORY © 2021 PORTAGE & MAIN PRESS ISBN: 978-1-77492-010-7

What Was It Like to Attend a Residential School?

TEACHER GUIDE FOR SUGAR FALLS: A RESIDENTIAL SCHOOL STORY © 2021 PORTAGE & MAIN PRESS ISBN:978-1-77492-010-7

DURATION

1–3 hours (1 hour to view and discuss videos as a class, 2 hours additional work time for optional project)

OVERVIEW

As a class, students will view one or more of the videos available on the web page "In Their Own Words."

BEFORE YOU BEGIN

- It is recommended that students complete this activity only after they've completed the Set Wellness Goals Using the Medicine Wheel activity on page 15 and have learned about wellness.

- Review the videos on "In Their Own Words," at <https://newsinteractives.cbc.ca/longform/residential-school-survivors>. Nine residential school Survivors talk about their experiences and the lasting impact these experiences had on their lives. These short videos range in length from approximately two to six minutes.

- Review Teaching Difficult Topics From a Trauma-Informed Stance in the introduction to this guide (page 6).

STEPS TO FOLLOW

- Prepare students before viewing the video(s):

  > Inform them that the material may be difficult to listen to and review their options for self-care. Remind students about resources that are available to them if they should feel overwhelmed or triggered at any point during this activity.

  > Advise students to keep in mind the fact that some of their own classmates may have relatives who've attended residential schools and to always be respectful and considerate of their classmates when learning about topics that affect students' lives.

- Have students view one or more of the videos available on "In Their Own Words," at <https://newsinteractives.cbc.ca/longform/residential-school-survivors>.

- Discuss why it's important for all Canadians to know this information. Common responses might include the following observations: to know your history, to know the history of the land you occupy, to gain understanding and empathy, to raise awareness of current issues, and to combat racism and misconceptions about Indigenous peoples.

- Follow-up project (optional): Have students showcase their learning in a way that can teach others (e.g., blog post, published essay, website). Have students co-construct the rubric for their projects. Criteria could include evidence of insight, incorporation of specific details from the videos, and presentation.

ASSESSMENT

Formative: Assess participation in whole-class discussion.

Summative: If students are assigned follow-up projects, formally grade their projects according to the co-constructed criteria.

TEACHER GUIDE FOR SUGAR FALLS: A RESIDENTIAL SCHOOL STORY © 2021 PORTAGE & MAIN PRESS ISBN: 978-1-77492-010-7

ANALYZE CHILDREN'S ART

SUBJECT AREA CONNECTIONS

Social Studies / English Language Arts / Arts Education

GOAL OF THIS ACTIVITY

Students will analyze primary source documents in the form of art produced by children at a residential school.

TEACHER GUIDE FOR SUGAR FALLS: A RESIDENTIAL SCHOOL STORY © 2021 PORTAGE & MAIN PRESS   ISBN: 978-1-77492-010-7

How Does Artwork Convey Mood?

DURATION

1 hour

OVERVIEW

Students will view artwork created by students of residential schools, analyze the colours and images in the artwork, and discuss the mood of the paintings.

BEFORE YOU BEGIN

- Review "Analyzing Images," one of the strategies on the Facing History and Ourselves website, at <https://www.facinghistory.org/resource-library/teaching-strategies/analyzing-images>, for a clear overview of how to guide students through close analysis of an image.

- Review the article "There Is Truth Here: The Power of Art From Residential Schools on Display," by Emily McCarty, at <https://thetyee.ca/Culture/2019/04/04/Power-Art-Residential-Schools-Students-Tribute/>. This article features artwork created by children who attended residential school, from the Museum of Vancouver exhibition titled *There Is Truth Here: Creativity and Resilience in Children's Art From Indian Residential and Day Schools.*

- Review classroom technology available for this activity. You will need enough computers/tablets with internet access or enough printed copies of the article for students to work in pairs.

STEPS TO FOLLOW

- As a class, review how to analyze an image, using one of the images featured in the article "There Is Truth Here: The Power of Art From Residential Schools on Display," by Emily McCarty, at <https://thetyee.ca/Culture/2019/04/04/Power-Art-Residential-Schools-Students-Tribute/>. Then, prompting as necessary, discuss the following questions:

  1. What did the child paint?
  2. What is the subject matter?
  3. What object(s), animals, or people are represented here?

TEACHER GUIDE FOR SUGAR FALLS: A RESIDENTIAL SCHOOL STORY © 2021 PORTAGE & MAIN PRESS ISBN: 978-1-77492-010-7

TEACHER GUIDE FOR SUGAR FALLS: A RESIDENTIAL SCHOOL STORY © 2021 PORTAGE & MAIN PRESS ISBN: 978-1-77492-010-7

4. How are they positioned?

5. What can you say about size or placement? (Does the image fill the whole frame? Is one object in front of another? Are they arranged in a circle?)

6. What do you notice about the elements of the artwork? What shapes, colours, or textures do you observe?

7. What mood do these shapes, colours, and textures suggest?

8. What attitude towards the subject matter does this artwork suggest?

9. What do you admire about this artwork?

Note: Answers may vary: for instance, the colour blue could suggest serenity or depression. Encourage students to share their answers without worrying about being wrong. The important thing is to look closely and then back up their answers with specific details from the artwork.

- Explain to students that this artwork was created by a child who attended residential school. Discuss how their knowledge of that context might help them think about the artwork.

- Have students work in pairs. Assign each pair one piece of artwork from the article. Have each pair analyze their image using the same questions from the class discussion (see above).

- As a class, co-construct assessment criteria for presenting their analysis to the class. Prompt students to generate criteria that address both observation and analysis, such as the following:

  > identifies at least two colours
  > identifies the main subject matter
  > describes the placement or arrangement of the object(s) in the frame
  > describes at least two dominant shapes or textures
  > identifies the mood
  > connects mood to colour or other elements
  > identifies at least one quality to praise and gives reasons

- Then have each pair present their analysis to the class. Ask the class what other observations and analysis they can come up with for each artwork.

ASSESSMENT

Formative: Assess for evidence of understanding by observing and supporting pairs as they work. Encourage students to be specific in their observations and creative in their analysis, and ask them to attempt to answer every question even if they aren't sure of their answers.

Summative: Assess student presentations using the co-constructed criteria. Alternatively, have students evaluate each other's presentations using the co-constructed criteria.

RESEARCH ETHICS AND EXPERIMENTS CONDUCTED ON CHILDREN IN RESIDENTIAL SCHOOLS

SUBJECT AREA CONNECTIONS

Social Studies / Science / English Language Arts / Psychology

GOALS OF THESE ACTIVITIES

Students will be introduced to the importance of ethics in scientific experiments. They will also learn about the various experiments that were conducted on Indigenous children attending residential school by reading nonfiction articles about these experiments.

BEFORE YOU BEGIN

* Review classroom technology available for this activity. You will need enough computers/tablets with internet access or enough copies of the articles for students to work with both during class time.

* Listen to the UBC podcast "The Legacy of Nutritional Experiments in Residential Schools" (1:46:00), at <https://www.alumni.ubc.ca/podcasts/the-legacy-of-nutritional-experiments-in-residential-schools/>. This resource is background information for teachers and not meant to be shared with students. These resources are recommended for both teachers and students:

    > "CSL Research Toolkit: Research Ethics," at <https://www.canadianschoollibraries.ca/research-toolkit/ethics>. Advice for teacher-librarians considering human-subject research, from the Canadian School Libraries website

    > "Ethics in Scientific Research," (8:01), at <https://www.youtube.com/watch?v=nX4c3V23DZI>. Video explaining human-subject research ethics to high school students headed for university research

Both explain in a detailed but accessible way the issues that must be considered in assessing the ethics of research on human subjects.

TEACHER GUIDE FOR SUGAR FALLS: A RESIDENTIAL SCHOOL STORY © 2021 PORTAGE & MAIN PRESS ISBN: 978-1-77492-010-7

ACTIVITY

Research Ethics and Nutrition Experiments in Residential Schools

TEACHER GUIDE FOR SUGAR FALLS: A RESIDENTIAL SCHOOL STORY © 2021 PORTAGE & MAIN PRESS   ISBN:978-1-7492-010-7

DURATION

1.5 hours

OVERVIEW

Students will read and discuss articles about nutrition experiments on students in residential schools and assess the experiments in terms of research ethics.

STEPS TO FOLLOW

* Have the class brainstorm what the words *ethics* and *ethical* mean. Have students look up definitions of these words in a dictionary.

* Introduce the concept of *research ethics*. (Optional: Give students copies of the information sheet "CSL Research Toolkit: Research Ethics," at <https://www.canadianschoollibraries.ca/research-toolkit/ethics>, or have them watch the video "Ethics in Scientific Research" (8:01), at <https://www.youtube.com/watch?v=nX4c3V23DZI;>, and then have students take turns summarizing the information with a partner.) Explain that ethical research involving human subjects

  > minimizes risk or harm to the people involved. Explain that harm can be physical, psychological, social, or economic.

  > ensures that subjects can choose whether or not to participate and requires informed consent of the research subjects. Children cannot legally consent, and no consent that is coerced is ethical. Children in residential schools were vulnerable to the authority figures in the school, and for that reason were not really free to choose.

  > recruits or chooses subjects for scientifically valid reasons according to principles of fairness and equity. "Race … should not be the basis for inclusion or exclusion as research subjects unless … specifically relevant to the purpose of the research."[10]

10 "CSL Research Toolkit: Research Ethics," Canadian School Libraries, accessed 7 June 2021, <https://www.canadianschoollibraries.ca/research-toolkit/ethics/>.

- Inform students that many residential school Survivors had long-term health issues due to nutrition experiments that were conducted in at least two schools. Some of the experiments involved decreasing food intake or withholding supplements. Even as children died, the experiments continued.

- Have students read the articles "Canada's Shameful History of Nutrition Research on Residential School Children: The Need for Strong Medical Ethics in Aboriginal Health Research," by Noni E. MacDonald, Richard Stanwick, and Andrew Lynk, at <https://www.ncbi.nlm.nih.gov/pmc/articles/PMC3941673/>, and "Residential School Nutrition Experiments Explained to Kenora Survivors," by Jody Porter, at <https://www.cbc.ca/news/canada/thunder-bay/residential-school-nutrition-experiments-explained-to-kenora-survivors-1.3171557>.

- For each article, have students work in pairs or individually to write responses to the following questions:

    1. Who was involved in the study? When did it take place?
    2. What was the purpose of the study?
    3. What are some possible long-term effects of the study?
    4. What questions do you have?
    5. What is your reaction to reading about this?

- Have students work in groups to create a poster or a presentation that evaluates one of these studies in terms of research ethics. The presentation should clearly address each of these criteria for ethical research on human subjects:

    > Minimal Risk (What physical, mental, social, or economic harms did the experiment risk?)

    > Consent (Were the children informed of the experiment and the risks involved? Were their parents/guardians informed? Were the children free to choose whether or not they were experimented on?)

    > Fairness and Equity (Why was this research conducted only on Indigenous children? Was this a scientifically valid reason for recruiting experimental subjects?)

ASSESSMENT

Summative: Assess written answers to questions 1 through 3 above for factual understanding; assess written answers to questions 3 through 5 for thoughtfulness. Assess answers for evidence of understanding of ethical research, ability to apply the criteria appropriately to the experiment they read about, and effectiveness of presentation (language).

TEACHER GUIDE FOR SUGAR FALLS: A RESIDENTIAL SCHOOL STORY © 2021 PORTAGE & MAIN PRESS ISBN: 978-1-77492-010-7

TEACHER GUIDE FOR SUGAR FALLS: A RESIDENTIAL SCHOOL STORY © 2021 PORTAGE & MAIN PRESS ISBN:978-1-77492-010-7

ACTIVITY

Read About Other Experiments on Children in Residential Schools

DURATION

1 hour

OVERVIEW

As a follow-up to the previous activity, students will read and discuss articles about other experiments done on students in residential schools.

BEFORE YOU BEGIN

* Review classroom technology available for this activity. You will need enough computers/ tablets with internet access or enough printed copies of the articles for students to work with both during class time.

STEPS TO FOLLOW

* Have students read the following articles:

    > "Ear Experiments Done on Kids at Kenora Residential School," by Jody Porter, at <https://www.cbc.ca/news/canada/thunder-bay/ ear-experiments-done-on-kids-at-kenora-residential-school-1.1343992>

    > "Psychic Experiments on First Nations Students Part of Unearthed Residential School History, Says Research Centre Director," by Jorge Barrera, at <https://www.aptnnews.ca/national-news/psychic-experiments-first-nation-students-part-unearthed-residential-school-history-says-research-centre-director/>

- For each article, have students work in pairs or individually to write responses to the following prompts:

    1. Who was involved in the study? When did it take place?
    2. What was the purpose of the study?
    3. Discuss the ethics involved in the study, with a focus on how this study would be considered unethical today.
    4. What are the similarities and differences between this study and the nutrition studies you read about in the previous activity?
    5. What are some possible long-term effects of the study?
    6. What is your reaction to reading about this?

ASSESSMENT

Summative: Assess written answers to questions 1 through 4 for factual understanding; assess written answers to questions 4 through 6 for thoughtfulness. Assess answers for evidence of understanding of ethical research, ability to apply the criteria appropriately to the experiment they read about, and effectiveness of presentation (language).

TEACHER GUIDE FOR SUGAR FALLS: A RESIDENTIAL SCHOOL STORY © 2021 PORTAGE & MAIN PRESS ISBN: 978-1-77492-010-7

TEACHER GUIDE FOR SUGAR FALLS: A RESIDENTIAL SCHOOL STORY © 2021 PORTAGE & MAIN PRESS   ISBN: 978-1-77492-010-7

WHOLE-SCHOOL ACTIVITIES

- Learn About Indigenous Culture and History

TEACHER GUIDE FOR SUGAR FALLS: A RESIDENTIAL SCHOOL STORY © 2021 PORTAGE & MAIN PRESS ISBN: 978-1-77492-010-7

LEARN ABOUT INDIGENOUS CULTURE AND HISTORY

TEACHER GUIDE FOR SUGAR FALLS: A RESIDENTIAL SCHOOL STORY © 2021 PORTAGE & MAIN PRESS   ISBN: 978-1-77492-010-7

SUBJECT AREA CONNECTIONS

Social Studies / English Language Arts

GOAL OF THESE ACTIVITIES

The following activities are engaging ways for the whole school to learn about Indigenous history and culture. Students do not need any background information about Indigenous topics to be able to benefit from the activities (nor do they need to be reading *Sugar Falls*). Rather, these activities serve to build community and allyship with Indigenous peoples. Consider asking your administration to dedicate one day per year for a whole-school activity to learn about an Indigenous topic.

Organize Orange Shirt Day for 30 September

DURATION

2 hours or longer (depending on class and school goals)

OVERVIEW

Orange Shirt Day is held each year on 30 September to witness and honour the healing journey of residential school Survivors.[11] We wear orange to stand with residential school Survivor Phyllis Webstad, whose orange shirt her grandma gave to her was taken away and replaced with a school uniform on her first day at a residential school—a metaphor for how residential schools stripped Indigenous children of their cultural identities and family connections. The National Centre for Truth and Reconciliation hosts an Orange Shirt Day event each year.

STEPS TO FOLLOW

* On Orange Shirt Day, have your class view the two videos found on the National Centre for Truth and Reconciliation's web page "Every Child Matters: Reconciliation Through Education," at <https://nctr.ca/education/every-child-matters/>. At time of printing, these are "Every Child Matters: Truth—Act One" (46:31) and "Every Child Matters: Reconciliation—Act Two" (48:29).

    Note: Videos are usually updated yearly. You can watch previous years' videos, or you can register your class to watch the event live each year.

* Have students write a reflection based on the videos they watched. Have them write about what stood out to them the most, how they felt about the topics discussed in the videos, and what they can do to advocate for change.

ASSESSMENT (OPTIONAL)

Summative: You may assess the written reflection for evidence of learning and for evidence of application of learning in generating ideas for change, depending on the goals of the class.

TEACHER GUIDE FOR SUGAR FALLS: A RESIDENTIAL SCHOOL STORY © 2021 PORTAGE & MAIN PRESS ISBN: 978-1-77492-010-7

---

[11] "The Story of Orange Shirt Day", Orange Shirt Society, accessed 7 June 2021, <http://www.orangeshirtday.org/about-us.html>.

Create a Living Library

TEACHER GUIDE FOR SUGAR FALLS: A RESIDENTIAL SCHOOL STORY © 2021 PORTAGE & MAIN PRESS ISBN: 978-1-77492-010-7

DURATION
1 hour per class (classes take turns throughout the day)

OVERVIEW
The "Living Library" (or the "Human Library") is an initiative that started in Copenhagen, Denmark, in 2000 to "encourage empathy and understanding where 'readers' can 'check out' an individual to hear their story."[12] A Living Library aims to break down prejudice and barriers between individuals who might not normally have a conversation. This activity adapts the Living Library idea as a whole-school initiative to learn from residential school Survivors.

STEPS TO FOLLOW

- Invite three to five residential school Survivors (or intergenerational Survivors) to visit your school. See Inviting an Elder Into Your Learning Space in the introduction to this guide (page 9) for useful guidelines on how to proceed.

- Organize 10- to 20-minute sessions, where each speaker shares their story with a class or small group of students throughout the day. Arrange for speakers to travel between classes, or have students go to different rooms to hear different speakers. Be sure to limit the number of sessions for each speaker (perhaps a maximum of three), agreeing to this number with the speaker ahead of time. Plan for time between sessions for the speaker to rest and recharge, and have videos available for backup in case a speaker needs a longer break than planned.

- Ensure guest speakers are appropriately compensated and thanked. Consider designating one student per class to give the guest tobacco (or another culturally appropriate acknowledgement) before they present to the class.

ASSESSMENT (OPTIONAL)
No assessment is required.

12 A. L., "The Human Library Organisation Replaces Pages With People," *The Economist*, 3 November 2017, <https://www.economist.com/prospero/2017/11/03/the-human-library-organisation-replaces-pages-with-people>.

WHILE READING
SUGAR FALLS

TEACHER GUIDE FOR SUGAR FALLS: A RESIDENTIAL SCHOOL STORY © 2021 PORTAGE & MAIN PRESS ISBN: 978-1-77492-010-7

TEACHER GUIDE FOR SUGAR FALLS: A RESIDENTIAL SCHOOL STORY © 2021 PORTAGE & MAIN PRESS ISBN: 978-1-77492-010-7

ENGAGING WITH THE TEXT

This section provides reading prompts and discussion questions to give students context and help them engage while they are reading *Sugar Falls*. The prompts are organized sequentially with activities that can be done as students progress through the book. Depending on your class, these prompts and discussions can be completed during class time or as homework, orally or in writing. Additionally, you may choose to assign students a reading journal where they can record their answers.

- Read and Respond to the Foreword

- Read and Respond to the Flashback

- Read and Respond to the Final Section of the Book

- Read and Respond to the Afterword

TEACHER GUIDE FOR SUGAR FALLS: A RESIDENTIAL SCHOOL STORY © 2021 PORTAGE & MAIN PRESS ISBN: 978-1-77492-010-7

READ AND RESPOND TO THE FOREWORD

TEACHER GUIDE FOR SUGAR FALLS: A RESIDENTIAL SCHOOL STORY © 2021 PORTAGE & MAIN PRESS   ISBN: 978-1-77492-010-7

SUBJECT AREA CONNECTIONS

English Language Arts / Social Studies / Arts Education

GOALS OF THIS ACTIVITY

Students read the foreword of *Sugar Falls* for information about the purpose, setting, and situation of the story, to make personal reflections on this information, and to make predictions about the story.

TEACHER GUIDE FOR SUGAR FALLS: A RESIDENTIAL SCHOOL STORY © 2021 PORTAGE & MAIN PRESS   ISBN: 978-1-77492-010-7

ACTIVITY

What Can We Expect From This Story?

DURATION

1 hour

OVERVIEW

Students will discuss the foreword with specific reference to details in the text.

STEPS TO FOLLOW

- Have students read Hon. Murray Sinclair's discussion on the power of "telling our stories." Then discuss the following questions as a class:

  > What does he mean by the power of "telling our stories"? (This question asks students to paraphrase.)

  > What are some ways in which stories "change us forever," according to Hon. Murray Sinclair?

  > What does Hon. Murray Sinclair hope will happen once people "collectively understand how things happened"?

  > Share an example of a story that changed you forever. How did this story impact you?

- Have students review pages 1–5 in *Sugar Falls*. Then have them answer the following questions. This may be done individually, in pairs, or as a class, in writing or orally:

  > What is the setting of the story? How do you know?

  > What clues do the author and illustrator use to convey the setting?

  > What do you learn from this section about the four sacred medicines?

  > What do you learn about the tobacco offering?

  > Why do you think the teacher includes these instructions in the assignment?

  > How does Daniel initially feel about the residential school assignment? How can you tell?

  > On page 2, April says, "No worries. Besides, I've always wondered about it, too." What can you infer from this?

- Have students flip through the remaining pages and look for examples of the Cree language. Have them share their discoveries with the rest of the class.

- Then have them answer the following question: Why do you think the author includes Cree language throughout the story?

ASSESSMENT

Formative: Observe and support students during discussion to assess evidence of their understanding.

Summative: Assess written answers for completeness and for evidence of students' ability to back up their answers with specific references to the text.

TEACHER GUIDE FOR SUGAR FALLS: A RESIDENTIAL SCHOOL STORY © 2021 PORTAGE & MAIN PRESS ISBN: 978-1-77492-010-7

READ AND RESPOND TO THE FLASHBACK

SUBJECT AREA CONNECTIONS

English Language Arts / Social Studies / Arts Education

GOALS OF THIS ACTIVITY

Students will read the flashback (pages 6–37) about the experiences April's kōkom had in residential school for information about her experiences and how they made her feel. Students will also analyze the flashback for its significance within *Sugar Falls* as a whole.

TEACHER GUIDE FOR SUGAR FALLS: A RESIDENTIAL SCHOOL STORY © 2021 PORTAGE & MAIN PRESS ISBN: 978-1-77492-010-7

Read and Reflect on the Residential School Experience of April's kōkom

DURATION:

1 hour

OVERVIEW

Students will read the words and images in the flashback for information about what happened to April's grandmother (Betsy) when she was sent to residential school and how those experiences affected her.

STEPS TO FOLLOW

* Have students respond to some or all of the following questions. Questions may be answered individually, in pairs, or as a class, in writing or orally.

    > Why do you think the Round Room provides April's kōkom with a sense of safety? How do you know?

    > On page 6, April's kōkom explains, in reference to her mother, "What I didn't know then was that she was a Survivor of a residential school and its unimaginable abuses." What can we infer from this about the way April's great-grandmother (Betsy's mother) may have been treated in residential school?

    > When the priest comes to take Betsy away, the colours of the images change. How does the illustrator use colour to convey the emotions Betsy and her family were feeling during this time?

    > April's kōkom compares the feeling she had when the priest took her to the feeling she had while abandoned under the canoe. How are these events similar?

    > Previously, on page 13, Betsy's father explained, "The beat of the drum represents the strength in our relationships with our ancestors, with our traditions, with Mother Earth, and with each other." How did the residential school system attempt to sever these relationships? Give specific examples from the flashback section of the text.

> What was daily life like for Betsy in residential school? How does this compare to what a high-quality school would be like? Give specific examples.

> How did Betsy resist assimilation at residential school? How did other children try to resist? Give specific examples.

> What were some coping mechanisms Betsy used to help her survive the trauma she endured? Give specific examples.

> What was the turning point in the story? Give reasons for your answer.

> How does the flashback enhance your understanding of the story?

ASSESSMENT

Formative: Observe and support students during discussion to assess evidence of their understanding.

Summative: Assess written answers for completeness and for evidence of students' ability to back up their answers with specific references to the text.

TEACHER GUIDE FOR SUGAR FALLS: A RESIDENTIAL SCHOOL STORY © 2021 PORTAGE & MAIN PRESS ISBN: 978-1-77492-010-7

READ AND RESPOND TO THE FINAL SECTION OF THE BOOK

TEACHER GUIDE FOR SUGAR FALLS: A RESIDENTIAL SCHOOL STORY © 2021 PORTAGE & MAIN PRESS ISBN: 978-1-77492-010-7

SUBJECT AREA CONNECTIONS

English Language Arts / Social Studies

GOALS OF THIS ACTIVITY

Students will read the final section of *Sugar Falls* (pages 38–40) for information about why Betty told her granddaughter her story and to reflect on why the story matters to April and to us.

Why Did April's kōkom Share Her Story?

TEACHER GUIDE FOR SUGAR FALLS: A RESIDENTIAL SCHOOL STORY © 2021 PORTAGE & MAIN PRESS ISBN: 978-1-77492-010-7

DURATION

1 hour

OVERVIEW

Students will locate the information in the book and explain why Betty told her story. Students will also reflect on why this story and similar stories are important.

STEPS TO FOLLOW

- Have students respond to some or all of the following questions. Questions may be answered individually, in pairs, or as a class, in writing or orally. What other questions would you ask Betty if you had the chance?

- On page 40, Betty explains why she chose to tell her story. What are her hopes?

- How can we work together to make sure that Betty's wishes come true?

- How can you be an ally and help share this message of hope?

- Why do you think the author decided to title the story "Sugar Falls"?

- Have you read other stories similar to this one? Which ones? How are they similar? How are they different?

ASSESSMENT

Formative: Observe and support students during discussion to assess evidence of their understanding.

Summative: Assess written answers for completeness and for evidence of students' ability to back up their answers with specific references to the text.

READ AND RESPOND TO THE AFTERWORD

SUBJECT AREA CONNECTIONS

English Language Arts / Physical Education / Health Education

GOAL OF THIS ACTIVITY

In her afterword, Elder Betty Ross talks about the sources of her strength being her Cree identity and language. Throughout this lesson, students will be encouraged to develop an understanding of their own sources of strength to promote wellness throughout their lives.

Find Your Sources of Strength

DURATION

1 hour

OVERVIEW

Students will engage in small-group discussions about resiliency and then create mind maps detailing their sources of strength. Finally, students will write a letter to themselves detailing their sources of strength.

STEPS TO FOLLOW

- Inform students that today's lesson will revolve around the topic of *resilience*. Ask if anyone can define *resilience*. If not, define it for them. According to the *Merriam-Webster Dictionary*, resilience is "an ability to recover from or adjust easily to misfortune or change."

- Divide students into groups of three or four. Pose a series of questions that groups will spend two to three minutes discussing.

  1. Why do you think it's important to be resilient? What are some life events that might happen where people could benefit from being resilient?
  2. What can Betty's life teach us about resiliency?
  3. What did Betty say are some of her sources of strength that helped her overcome the trauma she experienced at residential school?
  4. What are some of your sources of strength? How are they similar to or different from Betty's?

- Next, solicit answers from students about their sources of strength. Create a list of students' answers on the board. From the list, see if students can identify a few major themes or categories of sources of strength. Examples may include connection with others, healthy living habits, connection to culture.

- Have students create a Sources of Strength Mind Map where they identify the sources of their strength using both words and images. See "What Is a Mind Map?," at <https://www.mindmapping.com/mind-map>.

TEACHER GUIDE FOR SUGAR FALLS: A RESIDENTIAL SCHOOL STORY © 2021 PORTAGE & MAIN PRESS ISBN: 978-1-77492-010-7

- Finally, invite students to write a letter to their future selves, detailing their sources of strength and how they can use them to recover after a difficult experience. Before students begin, review the components of a letter, if needed.

ASSESSMENT

Since this assignment is highly personal, it is often difficult to grade.

Formative: Assess if students are engaged and participating in the small-group discussions.

Summative: Assess the letter for required components, completeness, and thoughtfulness.

BEYOND THE TEXT: SUGGESTIONS FOR FURTHER RESEARCH

The activities in this section serve to extend and enrich students' understanding of the information conveyed by or referred to in *Sugar Falls*. Having students do these activities while they are reading the book will enhance comprehension and engagement. Ensure that students know how to choose appropriate resources when conducting research.

- Learn About Other Indigenous People's Stories

TEACHER GUIDE FOR SUGAR FALLS: A RESIDENTIAL SCHOOL STORY © 2021 PORTAGE & MAIN PRESS   ISBN: 978-1-77492-010-7

LEARN ABOUT OTHER INDIGENOUS PEOPLE'S STORIES

TEACHER GUIDE FOR SUGAR FALLS: A RESIDENTIAL SCHOOL STORY © 2021 PORTAGE & MAIN PRESS   ISBN: 978-1-77492-010-7

SUBJECT AREA CONNECTIONS

English Language Arts / Social Studies

GOAL OF THESE ACTIVITIES

Students will develop and apply their independent research skills to learn more about the Indigenous people they encounter in the pages of *Sugar Falls* or in their communities.

Note: Before beginning either of these activities, review Teaching Difficult Topics From a Trauma-Informed Stance in the introduction to this guide (page 6). Inform students about resources that are available to them if they should feel overwhelmed or triggered at any point during this activity.

Research the Life of Hon. Murray Sinclair

DURATION

2–3 hours

OVERVIEW

Students will research the life of Hon. Murray Sinclair—the first Indigenous judge appointed in Manitoba, and only the second in Canada. Students will use sources on the internet to conduct their research.

STEPS TO FOLLOW

Assign students the task of researching Hon. Murray Sinclair's life and writing a short biography about his life and legacy.

ASSESSMENT

Summative: Assess students' writing and research skills according to the goals of the class. Consider co-constructing assessment criteria.

TEACHER GUIDE FOR SUGAR FALLS: A RESIDENTIAL SCHOOL STORY © 2021 PORTAGE & MAIN PRESS ISBN: 978-1-77492-010-7

Research the Life and Death of Helen Betty Osborne

TEACHER GUIDE FOR SUGAR FALLS: A RESIDENTIAL SCHOOL STORY © 2021 PORTAGE & MAIN PRESS ISBN: 978-1-77492-010-7

DURATION

2–3 hours (6–9 hours if also viewing the optional film)

OVERVIEW

April and Betty mention Helen Betty Osborne, a young Indigenous woman who was murdered in The Pas, Manitoba. Students will research her life and death and the reasons why it took so long for her murderers to be brought to justice. Students will then write a short report on what they have learned.

STEPS TO FOLLOW

* Optional: Have students view the two-part television miniseries *Conspiracy of Silence* (180:00) or read the graphic novel *Betty: The Helen Betty Osborne Story* by David A. Robertson.

* Have students research and write a short paper about the life and death of Helen Betty Osborne, and the subsequent murder investigation, with emphasis on the unequal treatment of her case by police.

* Before students begin their research and writing, have them co-create the criteria for assessment. Criteria could reference research (resources and information), analysis (logic and insight), organization (structure, transitions), argument (effectiveness, thesis), or language.

ASSESSMENT

Summative: Assess students' papers according to the co-constructed criteria.

Research the Issue of Missing and Murdered Indigenous Women and Girls (MMIWG)

DURATION

2–3 hours

OVERVIEW

Students will research Missing and Murdered Indigenous Women and Girls to understand the problem, including how the residential school system contributed to it.

BEFORE YOU BEGIN

Familiarize yourself with *Reclaiming Power and Place: The Final Report of the National Inquiry Into Missing and Murdered Indigenous Women and Girls*, available at <www.mmiwg-ffada.ca>. This website also has links to Key Moment Videos (at <https://www.mmiwg-ffada.ca/video-clips/>) as well as information about the Truth Sharing Podcasts (at <https://www.mmiwg-ffada.ca/wp-content/uploads/2019/05/News-Release-The-Truth-Sharing-Podcasts-ENG.pdf>).

STEPS TO FOLLOW

- Have students research the issue of Missing and Murdered Indigenous Women and Girls (MMIWG) with a focus on understanding the root causes of this problem, including ways in which the residential school system contributed to it.

- Ensure students draw from both the MMIWG report as well as women's stories. Stories can be found by viewing CBC's "Missing & Murdered: The Unsolved Cases of Indigenous Women and Girls" project, at <https://www.cbc.ca/missingandmurdered/>. Alternatively, students may draw on stories from the documentary series *Taken*, at <https://www.takentheseries.com/about/>.

TEACHER GUIDE FOR SUGAR FALLS: A RESIDENTIAL SCHOOL STORY © 2021 PORTAGE & MAIN PRESS ISBN: 978-1-77492-010-7

- Before students begin their research and writing, have them co-create the criteria for assessment. Criteria could reference research (resources and information), analysis (logic and insight), effectiveness of organization (structure, transitions), argument (effectiveness, thesis), or language.

- Have students present their research findings and analysis to the class.

ASSESSMENT

Summative: Assess students' papers according to the co-constructed criteria.

TEACHER GUIDE FOR SUGAR FALLS: A RESIDENTIAL SCHOOL STORY © 2021 PORTAGE & MAIN PRESS ISBN: 978-1-77492-010-7

Learn From Other Residential School Survivors

DURATION

1–2 hours

OVERVIEW

Students will listen to stories from other residential school Survivors using the Legacy of Hope archive. The Legacy of Hope Foundation is a national Indigenous charitable organization whose mandate is to increase awareness and knowledge of Canada's residential school system. The *Our Stories…Our Strength* archive consists of over 800 stories from residential school Survivors, 59 of which are available for free on their web page, "Residential School Survivor Stories."

Students will be exposed to stories from residential school Survivors, and then they will compare and contrast these stories to Betty's in *Sugar Falls*.

BEFORE YOU BEGIN

- Review the stories available from the Legacy of Hope archive on their web page, "Residential School Survivor Stories," at <https://legacyofhope.ca/wherearethechildren/stories/>. This website offers 59 videos, ranging in length from less than fifteen minutes to nearly an hour, of residential school Survivors telling their stories.

- Review Teaching Difficult Topics From a Trauma-Informed Stance in the introduction to this guide (page 6).

STEPS TO FOLLOW

- Prepare students before viewing video(s): Inform them that the material may be difficult to listen to, and review their options for self-care. Inform students about resources that are available to them if they should feel overwhelmed or triggered at any point during this activity.

TEACHER GUIDE FOR SUGAR FALLS: A RESIDENTIAL SCHOOL STORY © 2021 PORTAGE & MAIN PRESS ISBN: 978-1-77492-010-7

- Then either show students selected videos as a class, or assign selected videos for students to watch individually. Have students make notes about the experiences of the residential school Survivors whose stories they are hearing.

- Have students choose the stories of two residential school Survivors and then use their notes to write a compare-and-contrast essay about the similarities and differences in their experiences and Betty's experiences in *Sugar Falls*.

ASSESSMENT

Summative: Assess students' papers according to their content (specific information from the two stories), their analysis (logic and insight), their organization (compare and contrast), and the effectiveness of their presentation (language). Base criteria on the specifics of your assignment and the learning goals of your class. Consider co-constructing assessment criteria with the class.

TEACHER GUIDE FOR SUGAR FALLS: A RESIDENTIAL SCHOOL STORY © 2021 PORTAGE & MAIN PRESS ISBN: 978-1-77492-010-7

Learn From an Elder or Knowledge Keeper in Your Community

DURATION

1–2 hours

OVERVIEW

Inviting a local Elder or Knowledge Keeper into the classroom to talk about Indigenous culture serves to expose students to the positive aspects of Indigenous identity including language, culture, traditions, and beliefs. Students will gain an understanding of and appreciation for Indigenous culture.

Note: This activity is especially recommended if you do not plan to invite an Elder or Knowledge Keeper into your classroom later in the unit (see Part 3: After Reading *Sugar Falls*).

BEFORE YOU BEGIN

Review Inviting an Elder Into Your Learning Space in the introduction to this guide (page 9).

STEPS TO FOLLOW

If possible, determine ahead of time which protocols are recommended in your community. Prepare to spend time planning the visit. Have a list of possible topics to share with the Elder but also be prepared to listen and learn from the Elder as you invite their suggestions for presentation topics. After the Elder's visit, ensure that they are thanked and compensated appropriately.

ASSESSMENT (OPTIONAL)

No assessment is necessary.

Summative: If desired, have students write a reflection based on their experience learning from an Indigenous Elder or Knowledge Keeper. Assess according to the goals of the class.

TEACHER GUIDE FOR SUGAR FALLS: A RESIDENTIAL SCHOOL STORY © 2021 PORTAGE & MAIN PRESS ISBN: 978-1-77492-010-7

TEACHER GUIDE FOR SUGAR FALLS: A RESIDENTIAL SCHOOL STORY © 2021 PORTAGE & MAIN PRESS   ISBN: 978-1-77492-010-7

TEACHER GUIDE FOR SUGAR FALLS: A RESIDENTIAL SCHOOL STORY © 2021 PORTAGE & MAIN PRESS ISBN: 978-1-77492-010-7

AFTER READING *SUGAR FALLS*

The activities in this section serve to extend and expand students' understanding of the information conveyed by or referred to in *Sugar Falls*. Having students do these activities after they have read the book in its entirety will pull together students' understanding from previous activities and their reading experience.

TEACHER GUIDE FOR SUGAR FALLS: A RESIDENTIAL SCHOOL STORY © 2021 PORTAGE & MAIN PRESS ISBN: 978-1-77492-010-7

ENGAGING WITH THE TEXT

This section includes a variety of essay types and topic suggestions for students to complete a final writing assignment. Writing culminating novel-study essays is an effective way for students to practise their writing skills while developing their critical thinking skills by engaging with the themes and topics presented in the text.

* Respond to *Sugar Falls* With an Essay

TEACHER GUIDE FOR SUGAR FALLS: A RESIDENTIAL SCHOOL STORY © 2021 PORTAGE & MAIN PRESS ISBN: 978-1-77492-010-7

RESPOND TO *SUGAR FALLS* WITH AN ESSAY

SUBJECT AREA CONNECTIONS
English Language Arts / Social Studies

GOAL OF THIS ACTIVITY
Students revisit *Sugar Falls* and synthesize their understanding in an essay.

TEACHER GUIDE FOR SUGAR FALLS: A RESIDENTIAL SCHOOL STORY © 2021 PORTAGE & MAIN PRESS   ISBN: 978-1-77492-010-7

Write an Essay Based on Careful Reading

DURATION

1–3 hours

OVERVIEW

Students will review their knowledge of a particular essay genre (or of multiple essay genres) and apply that knowledge in an essay about *Sugar Falls*. Depending on students' backgrounds and the expectations for the class, one essay genre can be assigned, or students can choose among options.

BEFORE YOU BEGIN

- Determine which essay genre(s) you wish to emphasize in this activity, according to the goals and expectations of the class.

- Determine which question(s) you wish students to answer, using required essay genre(s). Here are some examples.

  ### NARRATIVE ESSAY

  > Write a narrative essay from the point of view of April's friend Daniel, explaining the story of your meeting with April's kōkom. Your teacher has asked you, "How does understanding the [residential school] system change your view of First Nations people?" What is your answer to this question—how has the experience of meeting April's kōkom and hearing her story changed you?

  > Write a narrative essay from the point of view of April's kōkom. What was it like for you to tell your story to April and Daniel, and why?

  > Betty Ross has shared her story with you. Perhaps you would like to share your story with her. Write a letter in the form of a narrative essay from your own point of view, in which you explain to Ms. Ross how reading *Sugar Falls* has changed your ideas about yourself and your community.

TEACHER GUIDE FOR SUGAR FALLS: A RESIDENTIAL SCHOOL STORY © 2021 PORTAGE & MAIN PRESS ISBN: 978-1-77492-010-7

DESCRIPTIVE ESSAY

> Compare and contrast young Betsy's environment with her family and her environment at the residential school. What are the most important differences?

> How does April's kōkom create a safe space for herself to tell her story? What are its most important features?

EXPOSITORY ESSAY

> Betsy learns how to be strong from her dad. What does Indigenous strength look like, according to *Sugar Falls*?

> What harms did the residential schools cause, according to *Sugar Falls*?

> Why did the author of this graphic novel, David A. Robertson, call it *Sugar Falls*? Explain what Sugar Falls symbolizes in the story and why the title is appropriate.

> How does Betty's story demonstrate resilience both personally and collectively?

PERSUASIVE ESSAY

> Write a letter to your principal or school board convincing them that *Sugar Falls* should be mandatory in all Grade 10 English (or Social Studies) classes.

> Write a letter to your Member of the Legislative Assembly detailing why you support the creation of a Task Force for Missing and Murdered Indigenous Women and Girls.

> Write a letter to your principal or school board convincing them to work towards implementing a call to action item from the TRC's *Calls to Action*.

STEPS TO FOLLOW

* Review the structures and conventions of the essay genre(s) to be assigned.

* Introduce the question(s) being assigned. If more than one question is being assigned, choose one to model the process with the class.

* As a class, brainstorm details from *Sugar Falls* that would help answer the assigned question. Then brainstorm a list of possible answers to the question (thesis statements).

* Explain the available options and requirements. Expectations may include such features as conventions of the assigned genre (style and structure), length, and minimum number of specific references to *Sugar Falls*. Consider co-constructing assessment criteria as a class.

ASSESSMENT

Summative: Assess completed papers based on the announced expectations and criteria. Consider holding writing conferences with students in which they self-assess.

BEYOND THE TEXT: SUGGESTIONS FOR FURTHER RESEARCH

The activities in this section serve to extend and enrich students' understanding of the information conveyed by or referred to in *Sugar Falls*. Having students do these activities after they have read the book will enhance understanding and promote application of what they have learned.

- Education for Change

- Learn About Creating Change Through Art

- Learn About Indigenous Cultures and Languages

- Culminating Project: Advocate for Change

TEACHER GUIDE FOR SUGAR FALLS: A RESIDENTIAL SCHOOL STORY © 2021 PORTAGE & MAIN PRESS ISBN: 978-1-77492-0107

EDUCATION FOR CHANGE

SUBJECT AREA CONNECTIONS

Social Studies / English Language Arts / Current Topics in First Nations, Métis, and Inuit Studies

GOAL OF THESE ACTIVITIES

Students will learn about recent and ongoing events that are important to our understanding of the history of residential schools and are important to our ongoing responses to this history.

TEACHER GUIDE FOR SUGAR FALLS: A RESIDENTIAL SCHOOL STORY © 2021 PORTAGE & MAIN PRESS   ISBN: 978-1-77492-010-7

Learn About the TRC's Final Report and Recommendations

DURATION

2–3 hours

OVERVIEW

Through reading one of the chapters in *Honouring the Truth, Reconciling for the Future: Summary of the Final Report of the Truth and Reconciliation Commission of Canada*, and the Truth and Reconciliation Commission (TRC)'s *Calls to Action*, students will gain deeper insight into the background, history, and legacy of residential schools as well as the outcome of the TRC.

BEFORE YOU BEGIN

Review the following information.

The Truth and Reconciliation Commission of Canada

- In 2000, five residential school Survivors launched a class-action lawsuit against the Canadian government for the abuses they suffered at residential school.[13] Thousands more lawsuits were added shortly after.

- The Truth and Reconciliation Commission of Canada was formed out of the Indian Residential Schools Settlement Agreement—the largest class-action settlement agreement in Canada[14]— in which the government set aside 1.9 billion dollars to help former students in their recovery.[15]

- The 2007 Indian Residential Schools Settlement Agreement had five components: the Common Experience Payment, Independent Assessment Process, the Truth and Reconciliation Commission, Commemoration, and Health and Healing Services.[16]

---

[13] "Ontario Natives Launch Residential School Lawsuit," *CBC News*, 20 June 2000, <https://www.cbc.ca/news/canada/ontario-natives-launch-residential-school-lawsuit-1.240548>.

[14] "About the Truth and Reconciliation Commission," Crown-Indigenous Relations and Northern Affairs Canada, Government of Canada, 4 June 2021, <https://www.rcaanc-cirnac.gc.ca/eng/1450124405592/1529106060525>.

[15] Tabitha Marshall, updated by David Joseph Gallant, "Indian Residential Schools Settlement Agreement," *Canadian Encyclopedia*, 16 January 2020, <https://www.thecanadianencyclopedia.ca/en/article/indian-residential-schools-settlement-agreement>.

[16] Ibid.

TEACHER GUIDE FOR SUGAR FALLS: A RESIDENTIAL SCHOOL STORY © 2021 PORTAGE & MAIN PRESS ISBN: 978-1-77492-010-7

- The Truth and Reconciliation Commission of Canada was responsible for hearing and documenting the testimonies of residential school Survivors.[17] The Canadian TRC is similar to South Africa's Truth and Reconciliation Commission, which was responsible for hearing and documenting the testimonies of people who lived under the Apartheid system in South Africa.[18]

- In 2008, then prime minister of Canada Stephen Harper made a Statement of Apology to former students of Indian Residential Schools, on behalf of the Government of Canada.[19]

- In 2015, the TRC released its final report along with 94 *Calls to Action* to "redress the legacy of residential schools and advance the process of Canadian reconciliation."[20] The TRC defines reconciliation as "an ongoing process of establishing and maintaining respectful relationships."[21]

STEPS TO FOLLOW

- Divide the class into groups of four or more students. Assign each group either one chapter of *Honouring the Truth, Reconciling for the Future: Summary of the Final Report of the Truth and Reconciliation Commission of Canada* ("The History"; "The Legacy"; or "The Challenge of Reconciliation"), at <https://web-trc.ca/>, or all of *Truth and Reconciliation Commission of Canada: Calls to Action*, at <https://ehprnh2mwo3.exactdn.com/wp-content/uploads/2021/01/Calls_to_Action_English2.pdf>.

- Within each group, have students divide up the readings so each student reads and summarizes a section within the chapter. Have group members share their summaries with one another to create a combined summary of the assigned reading's key points.

- Have each group create a presentation of their findings that includes visuals. Have students co-construct the presentation criteria before they start working on their presentations.

- Have each group share their presentation with the class so that the class can learn from each report.

ASSESSMENT

Summative: Assess individuals on summaries (accuracy and comprehensiveness); assess groups according to the co-constructed criteria.

---

[17] "About the Truth and Reconciliation Commission of Canada," Crown-Indigenous Relations and Northern Affairs Canada, Government of Canada, 4 June 2021, <https://www.rcaanc-cirnac.gc.ca/eng/1450124405592/1529106060525>.

[18] "Canada's Truth Commission Learned From Mandela, Says Head," *CBC News*, 7 December 2013, <https://www.cbc.ca/news/canada/manitoba/canada-s-truth-commission-learned-from-mandela-says-head-1.2454851>.

[19] "Statement of Apology to Former Students of Indian Residential Schools," Crown-Indigenous Relations and Northern Affairs Canada, Government of Canada, 15 September 2010, <https://www.rcaanc-cirnac.gc.ca/eng/1100100015644/1571589171655>.

[20] *Truth and Reconciliation Commission of Canada: Calls to Action* (Winnipeg: Truth and Reconciliation Commission of Canada, 2015), <https://ehprnh2mwo3.exactdn.com/wp-content/uploads/2021/01/Calls_to_Action_English2.pdf>.

[21] Truth and Reconciliation Commission of Canada, *Canada's Residential Schools: Reconciliation*, vol. 6 of *The Final Report of the Truth and Reconciliation Commission of Canada* (Montreal: McGill-Queen's University Press, 2015), 11, <https://ehprnh2mwo3.exactdn.com/wp-content/uploads/2021/01/Volume_6_Reconciliation_English_Web.pdf>.

TEACHER GUIDE FOR SUGAR FALLS: A RESIDENTIAL SCHOOL STORY © 2021 PORTAGE & MAIN PRESS ISBN: 978-1-77492-010-7

Complete an Inquiry Project About a Current Topic

TEACHER GUIDE FOR SUGAR FALLS: A RESIDENTIAL SCHOOL STORY © 2021 PORTAGE & MAIN PRESS ISBN: 978-1-77492-010-7

DURATION

4–5 hours

OVERVIEW

This student-led inquiry project encourages students to take ownership of their learning by choosing a topic they are interested in learning more about, researching that topic, and presenting their findings to the class. This project can be done individually or in groups.

BEFORE YOU BEGIN

Review the excellent materials available to support inquiry-based learning found on the Edutopia website, at <https://www.edutopia.org/article/inquiry-based-learning-resources-downloads>. "Creating a Culture of Inquiry," by Andrew Miller, at <https://www.edutopia.org/blog/creating-a-culture-of-inquiry-andrew-mille>, is also highly recommended.

STEPS TO FOLLOW

- Have students/groups brainstorm a list of current topics related to Indigenous people in Canada. Examples might include the child welfare system, day schools, Missing and Murdered Indigenous Women and Girls, land claims, Indigenous businesses, Indigenous resistance movements, etc. Encourage them to revisit *Sugar Falls* for ideas.

- Then have students select the topic they are most interested in.

- Have students select an open-ended research question that will guide their study. An open-ended question cannot be answered with yes or no. A good open-ended question often begins with *what*, *why*, or *how*. An example of an open-ended research question is "What are some of the most successful Indigenous businesses in Canada?"

- Once students have their research questions, have them begin researching all the possible answers to their question.

- Provide time (in class and/or for homework) for students to research their selected topic and write a research paper detailing their findings. Alternatively, depending on the goals and expectations of your class, students could do a creative project (e.g., video, artwork, comic strip, skit, screenplay) that conveys their findings or write a persuasive essay addressed to a particular audience who the student believes should take action based on their research.

Note: When assigning a research project, ensure that students know how to choose appropriate resources when conducting research.

ASSESSMENT

Summative: You may assess the inquiry question (open-ended and appropriate); you may assess the research process (number and quality of sources, good notes). Assess the final paper for content (information found through research), analysis (how well the inquiry question is answered), and presentation (how well it meets your expectations for organization, format, and language). Consider holding writing conferences with students in which they self-assess.

LEARN ABOUT CREATING CHANGE THROUGH ART

SUBJECT AREA CONNECTIONS

Arts Education / Social Studies / History / English Language Arts

GOAL OF THIS ACTIVITY

Through this lesson, students will be exposed to a social justice movement that raises awareness about Missing and Murdered Indigenous Women and Girls and Two-Spirit People. Students will reflect on the project and its potential impact.

Note: Although this activity can stand on its own, it can also be used to prepare students for the Culminating Project: Advocate for Change (page 82) if desired.

TEACHER GUIDE FOR SUGAR FALLS: A RESIDENTIAL SCHOOL STORY © 2021 PORTAGE & MAIN PRESS ISBN: 978-1-77492-010-7

Analyze the REDress Project

TEACHER GUIDE FOR SUGAR FALLS: A RESIDENTIAL SCHOOL STORY © 2021 PORTAGE & MAIN PRESS   ISBN: 978-1-77492-010-7

DURATION

1 hour

OVERVIEW

Students will view a video about artist Jaime Black's REDress Project and will reflect on how Black's work created awareness about Missing and Murdered Indigenous Women and Girls.

STEPS TO FOLLOW

- Ask students to brainstorm how art can create change. What are some examples of art creating change?

- Next, ask students what *redress* means. Have students look up *redress* in a dictionary and discuss examples. Explain that the REDress Project uses red dresses to create art designed to redress injustice.

- Show them the video "The REDress Project at the National Museum of the American Indian" (2:39), by Jaime Black, at <https://www.jaimeblackartist.com/exhibitions/>.

- As a class or in groups, have students discuss the goals of the REDress Project as explained on Black's website:

  > How does the project "draw attention to the gendered and racialized nature of violent crimes against Aboriginal women"?

  > How do the red dresses "evoke a presence through the marking of absence?

  > How effective is this project at changing attitudes or perceptions?

- Have students write a reflection on art's power to change attitudes or perceptions, including examples from the REDress project.

ASSESSMENT

Formative: Assess reflections for evidence of learning and thought. If using this activity to prepare for the Culminating Project: Advocate for Change (page 82), have students share their reflections in groups to compare ideas about how art can create change.

Summative: Assess for specific details, analysis, and writing skills.

TEACHER GUIDE FOR SUGAR FALLS: A RESIDENTIAL SCHOOL STORY © 2021 PORTAGE & MAIN PRESS   ISBN: 978-1-77492-010-7

LEARN ABOUT INDIGENOUS CULTURES AND LANGUAGES

TEACHER GUIDE FOR SUGAR FALLS: A RESIDENTIAL SCHOOL STORY © 2021 PORTAGE & MAIN PRESS   ISBN: 978-1-77492-010-7

SUBJECT AREA CONNECTIONS

Mathematics / Science / English Language Arts / Social Studies

GOAL OF THIS ACTIVITY

Students will be exposed to a positive aspect of Indigenous history and culture and develop appreciation for the strength and beauty in an Indigenous culture.

Note: This unit is especially recommended if you have not invited an Elder or Knowledge Keeper to visit your classroom earlier in the unit (see the activity Learn From a Knowledge Keeper or Elder on page 63).

Learn From an Elder or Knowledge Keeper

DURATION
1–2 hours

OVERVIEW
Students will learn about Indigenous cultures and languages from a local Elder or Knowledge Keeper.

BEFORE YOU BEGIN
Review Inviting an Elder Into Your Learning Space in the introduction to this guide (page 9).

STEPS TO FOLLOW

* If possible, determine ahead of time which protocols are recommended in your community. Prepare to spend time planning the visit.

    > Have a list of possible topics to share with the Elder. Ideas with curriculum connections include star teachings (science), beading (math), oral history (social studies), Indigenous languages (English language arts).

    > If you plan to assign the Culminating Project: Advocate for Change, consider inviting the Elder to teach about the power of Indigenous art or Indigenous story.

    > Remember to invite suggestions from the Elder or Knowledge Keeper for topics they feel comfortable teaching.

* After the Elder's visit, ensure that they are thanked and compensated appropriately.

ASSESSMENT (OPTIONAL)

Summative: If desired, have students write a reflection based on their experience learning from an Indigenous Elder or Knowledge Keeper. Assess according to the learning goals of your class.

TEACHER GUIDE FOR SUGAR FALLS: A RESIDENTIAL SCHOOL STORY © 2021 PORTAGE & MAIN PRESS ISBN: 978-1-77492-010-7

CULMINATING PROJECT: ADVOCATE FOR CHANGE

SUBJECT AREA CONNECTIONS

Global Issues: Citizenship and Sustainability/ Social Studies / Arts Education

GOAL OF THIS ACTIVITY

Students will take what they learned in this unit and apply it to a social justice action project of their choice.

TEACHER GUIDE FOR SUGAR FALLS: A RESIDENTIAL SCHOOL STORY © 2021 PORTAGE & MAIN PRESS ISBN: 978-1-77492-010-7

Complete a Social Justice Action Project

DURATION

4–5 hours

GOAL OF THIS ACTIVITY

Students will complete an original project that will achieve one of the following goals:

* raise awareness about an Indigenous topic
* fundraise for an organization supporting Indigenous peoples
* advocate for change
* recruit volunteers for an organization supporting Indigenous people

STEPS TO FOLLOW

* Have students (individually, in pairs, or in groups) choose a topic studied in this unit on which to base a social justice action project that will educate and raise awareness about the topic. Appropriate topics include the residential school system, the 60s Scoop, day schools, Missing and Murdered Indigenous Women and Girls and Two-Spirit People, and the child welfare system, among others.

* Have students conduct research into their topic, and then have students present their findings in a way that maximizes their presentation's effect on their audience. Depending on the goals of your course, criteria could emphasize the use of art to effect change (as explored in the REDress project) or the use of technology to reach as many people as possible (as with a social media campaign).

* As a class, co-construct assessment criteria.

ASSESSMENT

Summative: Assess final project on content and presentation according to the co-constructed assessment criteria.

TEACHER GUIDE FOR SUGAR FALLS: A RESIDENTIAL SCHOOL STORY © 2021 PORTAGE & MAIN PRESS   ISBN: 978-1-77492-010-7

TEACHER GUIDE FOR SUGAR FALLS: A RESIDENTIAL SCHOOL STORY   © 2021 PORTAGE & MAIN PRESS   ISBN: 978-1-77492-010-7

RESOURCES

RESOURCES FOR STUDENTS

BOOKS

Hill, Gord. *The 500 Years of Resistance Comic Book.* Foreword by Ward Churchill. Vancouver: Arsenal Pulp Press, 2010.

Robertson, David A. *Betty: The Helen Betty Osborne Story.* Illustrated by Scott B. Henderson. Winnipeg: HighWater Press, 2015.

———. *Sugar Falls: A Residential School Story.* Tenth Anniversary Edition. Winnipeg: HighWater Press, 2021.

WEBSITES AND ONLINE RESOURCES

Barrera, Jorge. "Psychic Experiments on First Nations Students Part of Unearthed Residential School History, Says Research Centre Director." *APTN National News*, 13 January 2015. https://www.aptnnews.ca/national-news/psychic-experiments-first-nation-students-part-unearthed-residential-school-history-says-research-centre-director/.

Black, Jaime. "The REDress Project at the National Museum of the American Indian." National Museum of the American Indian. Video, 2:39. https://www.jaimeblackartist.com/exhibitions/.

"Did You Live Near a Residential School?" *CBC News.* https://www.cbc.ca/news2/interactives/beyond-94-residential-school-map/.

TEACHER GUIDE FOR SUGAR FALLS: A RESIDENTIAL SCHOOL STORY © 2021 PORTAGE & MAIN PRESS ISBN: 978-1-77492-010-7

"Every Child Matters: Reconciliation Through Education." National Centre for Truth and Reconciliation. https://nctr.ca/education/every-child-matters/.

Register yourself or your class for the 30 September online event open to all Canadian schools, or view the videos "Every Child Matters: Truth – Act One" and "Every Child Matters: Reconciliation – Act Two."

"Heritage Minutes: Chanie Wenjack." Historica Canada. Video, 1:00. https://www.historicacanada.ca/content/heritage-minutes/chanie-wenjack.

This video tells the story of Chanie Wenjack, whose death sparked the first inquest into the treatment of Indigenous children in Canadian residential schools.

HighSchoolScience101. "Ethics in Scientific Research." YouTube video, 8:01. 1 July 2019. https://www.youtube.com/watch?v=nX4c3V23DZI.

Aimed at high school students who plan to conduct research in university. Explains the issues of risk and harm, consent, recruitment, and identifiability that must be considered in assessing the ethics of research on human subjects.

"Historic Treaties and Treaty First Nations in Canada Infographic." Crown-Indigenous Relations and Northern Affairs Canada. Government of Canada. 7 November 2013. https://www.rcaanc-cirnac.gc.ca/eng/1380223988016/1544125243779.

Indigenous Foundations. First Nations & Indigenous Studies, the University of British Columbia. https://indigenousfoundations.arts.ubc.ca/home.

"In Their Own Words." *CBC News*. 19 March 2018. https://newsinteractives.cbc.ca/longform/residential-school-survivors.

Nine residential school Survivors talk about their experiences and the lasting impact these experiences had on their lives. Short videos that range in length from 2:19 to 5:31.

MacDonald, Noni E., Richard Stanwick, and Andrew Lynk. "Canada's Shameful History of Nutrition Research on Residential School Children: The Need For Strong Medical Ethics in Aboriginal Health Research." *Paediatrics & Child Health* 19, no. 2 (February 2014): 64. https://www.ncbi.nlm.nih.gov/pmc/articles/PMC3941673/.

Mankieicz, Francis, dir. *Conspiracy of Silence*. CBC, 1991. Two-part miniseries, 180 min.

"Map of the Numbered Treaties." Treaty Relations Commission of Manitoba. http://www.trcm.ca/treaties/treaties-in-manitoba/view-pdf-interactive-map-of-numbered-treaties-trcm-july-20-entry/.

A downloadable PDF of the Manitoba Numbered Treaties Map in both English and French.

McCarty, Emily. "There Is Truth Here: The Power of Art from Residential Schools on Display." *The Tyee*, 4 April 2019. https://thetyee.ca/Culture/2019/04/04/Power-Art-Residential-Schools-Students-Tribute/.

Article describes and gives examples of images of artwork created by children who attended residential school, from the exhibition *There Is Truth Here* at the Museum of Vancouver.

"Missing & Murdered: The Unsolved Cases of Indigenous Women and Girls." *CBC News*. https://www.cbc.ca/missingandmurdered/.

M'Lot, Christine. "Medicine Wheel Goal Setting." YouTube video, 15:36. https://www.youtube.com/watch?v=0N9bI9FSbcA.

National Centre for Truth and Reconciliation Canada. University of Manitoba. http://nctr.ca/

Includes information on residential schools, history, and Indigenous resilience.

Native Land. Native Land Digital. https://native-land.ca.

"Ontario First Nations Maps." Government of Ontario. https:// www.ontario.ca/page/ ontario-first-nations-maps#section-0.

Porter, Jody. "Ear Experiments Done on Kids at Kenora Residential School." *CBC News*, 8 August 2013. https://www.cbc.ca/news/canada/thunder-bay/ear-experiments-done-on-kids-at-kenora-residential-school-1.1343992.

———. "Residential School Nutrition Experiments Explained to Kenora Survivors." *CBC News*, 29 July 2015. https://www.cbc.ca/news/canada/thunder-bay/ residential-school-nutrition-experiments-explained-to-kenora-survivors-1.3171557.

Project of Heart. Sylvia Smith. http://projectofheart.ca.

An educational tool kit designed to engage students in a deeper exploration of Indigenous traditions in Canada and the history of residential schools. It offers an inquiry-based, hands-on, collaborative, inter-generational, artistic journey.

"Residential Schools." National Film Board of Canada. https://www.nfb.ca/subjects/indigenous-peoples-in-canada-first-nations-and-metis/residential-schools/.

"Residential School Survivor Stories." Legacy of Hope Foundation. https://legacyofhope.ca/wherearethe children/stories/.

A selection of 59 Survivor stories drawn from the *Our Stories...Our Strength* video collection, ranging in length from less than fifteen minutes to nearly an hour. Links to 33 films about residential schools, ranging in length from 03:00 to 2:42:00.

Rifkind, Candida, and Brandon Christopher. *How Comics Work*. Illustrated by Alice RL. Winnipeg: Department of English, University of Winnipeg, 2019, uwinnipeg.ca/1B19. https://www.uwinnipeg. ca/1b19/docs/how-comics-work-web-cc-by-nc-nd.pdf.

Taken. Eagle Vision. https://www.takentheseries.com/about/.

Information about the documentary TV series *Taken*, created by Lisa Meeches, Kyle Irving, and Rebecca Gibson and produced by Eagle Vision Inc., which focuses on individual stories of Missing and Murdered Indigenous Women and Girls. To view the episodes you need an account with Lumi, APTN's new streaming service, but they do offer a one-month free trial, at https://aptnlumi.ca/#/auth/login.

Truth and Reconciliation Commission of Canada. *Honouring the Truth, Reconciling for the Future: Summary of the Final Report of the Truth and Reconciliation Commission of Canada*. https://www.web-trc.ca.

An unofficial plain-text extract of the original report, aimed at making the report more accessible.

———. *Truth and Reconciliation Commission of Canada: Calls to Action*. Winnipeg: Truth and Reconciliation Commission of Canada, 2015. https://ehprnh2mwo3.exactdn.com/wp-content/uploads/2021/01/ Calls_to_Action_English2.pdf.

"What Is a Mind Map?" *MindMapping.com*. https://www.mindmapping.com/mind-map.

TEACHER GUIDE FOR SUGAR FALLS: A RESIDENTIAL SCHOOL STORY © 2021 PORTAGE & MAIN PRESS ISBN:978-1-77492-010-7

RESOURCES FOR TEACHERS

BOOKS

Benn, Carl. *Mohawks on the Nile: Natives Among the Canadian Voyageurs in Egypt, 1884–1885*. Toronto: Dundurn Press, 2009.

Davidson, Sarah Florence, and Robert Davidson. *Potlatch as Pedagogy: Learning Through Ceremony*. Winnipeg: Portage & Main Press, 2018.

Fontaine, Phil, Aimée Craft, and the Truth and Reconciliation Commission of Canada. *A Knock on the Door: The Essential History of Residential Schools from the Truth and Reconciliation Commission of Canada*. Winnipeg: University of Manitoba, 2015.

Edited and abridged from reports of the Truth and Reconciliation Commission of Canada and the TRC's *Calls to Action*.

Katz, Jennifer, with Kevin Lamoureux. *Ensouling Our Schools: A Universally Designed Framework for Mental Health, Well-Being, and Reconciliation*. Winnipeg: Portage & Main Press, 2018.

Keoke, Emory Dean, and Kay Marie Porterfield. *Medicine and Health: American Indian Contributions to the World*. New York: Chelsea House, 2005.

A resource for chemistry classes. Go to any one of the three sections on plant medicines and have students select one of these medicines and identify the compounds in it. Extend this activity by exploring how similar modern medicines (and their compounds) can be harmful to the environment (e.g., ending up in the water table through improper disposal). Examine ways to provide medicines that leave a healthier footprint on the Earth.

———. *Science and Technology: American Indian Contributions to the World*. New York: Chelsea House, 2005.

A resource for classes on physics, light, and geometric optics. Go to the section on sound and light and have students identify the Indigenous knowledge and technologies related to light. Extend this activity by exploring how these scientific insights and innovations enhanced life for Indigenous people.

———. *Trade, Transportation and Warfare: American Indian Contributions to the World*. New York, Chelsea House, 2005.

Go to the section on transportation on water or transportation on land. Have students select one of these Indigenous technologies and explore Newton's laws of motion in relation to this technology.

King, Thomas. *The Inconvenient Indian: A Curious Account of Native People in North America*. Toronto: Penguin Random House Canada, 2012.

Niezen, Ronald. *Truth and Indignation: Canada's Truth and Reconciliation Commission on Indian Residential Schools*. 2nd ed. Toronto: University of Toronto Press, 2017.

Peterson, Shelley Stagg. *Teaching With Graphic Novels*. Winnipeg: Portage & Main Press, 2010.

Toulouse, Pamela Rose. *Achieving Indigenous Student Success: A Guide for Secondary Classrooms*. Winnipeg: Portage & Main Press, 2016.

———. *Truth and Reconciliation in Canadian Schools*. Winnipeg: Portage & Main Press, 2018.

Vowel, Chelsea. *Indigenous Writes: A Guide to First Nations, Métis & Inuit Issues in Canada*. Winnipeg: HighWater Press, 2016.

Wagamese, Richard. *Indian Horse*. Vancouver: Douglas & McIntyre, 2012.

WEBSITES AND ONLINE RESOURCES

"About the Truth and Reconciliation Commission." Crown-Indigenous Relations and Northern Affairs Canada. Government of Canada, 4 June 2021. https://www.rcaanc-cirnac.gc.ca/eng/1450124405592/1529106060525.

Al Jazeera English. *Canada's Dark Secret*. Documentary available on YouTube, 47:30. 13 June 2017. https://www.youtube.com/watch?v=peLd_jtMdrc.

"Analyzing Images." Facing History and Ourselves. https://www.facinghistory.org/resource-library/teaching-strategies/analyzing-images.

> A resource library with several teaching strategies useful in a history or social studies classroom. The website is dedicated to using "lessons of history to challenge teachers and their students to stand up to bigotry and hate."

Beaulieu, Kelly J. "The Seven Lessons of the Medicine Wheel." *Say Magazine*, 24 August 2018. https://saymag.com/the-seven-lessons-of-the-medicine-wheel/.

Butler, Lisa D., Filomena M. Critelli, and Elaine S. Rinfrette. "Trauma-Informed Care and Mental Health." *Directions in Psychiatry* 31, no. 3 (January 2011): 197–208. https://www.researchgate.net/publication/234155324_Trauma-Informed_Care_and_Mental_Health.

"Canada's Truth Commission Learned From Mandela, Says Head." *CBC News*, 7 December 2013. https://www.cbc.ca/news/canada/manitoba/canada-s-truth-commission-learned-from-mandela-says-head-1.2454851.

Carleton, Sean. "John A. Macdonald Was the Real Architect of Residential Schools." *Toronto Star*, 9 July 2017. https://www.thestar.com/opinion/commentary/2017/07/09/john-a-macdonald-was-the-real-architect-of-residential-schools.html.

"CSL Research Toolkit: Research Ethics." *Canadian School Libraries*. https://www.canadianschoollibraries.ca/research-toolkit/ethics/.

"Education." National Centre for Truth and Reconciliation. University of Manitoba. https://nctr.ca/education/.

"Educators." Indspire. https://indspire.ca/programs/educators/

"First Nations in Canada." Crown-Indigenous Relations and Northern Affairs Canada. Government of Canada, 2 May 2017. https://www.rcaanc-cirnac.gc.ca/eng/1307460755710/1536862806124.

Indian Residential Schools & Reconciliation: Teacher Resource Guide. Vancouver: First Nations Education Steering Committee, 2015. http://www.fnesc.ca/grade-10irsr/.

"An Interactive Lesson Plan for Teaching Students How to Set S.M.A.R.T. Goals." *TeacherVision* (blog), 17 January 2019. https://www.teachervision.com/blog/morning-announcements/an-interactive-lesson-plan-for-teaching-students-how-to-set-smart-goals.

The Jigsaw Classroom. Social Psychology Network, 2021. https://www.jigsaw.org.

"Key Moment Videos." National Inquiry Into Missing and Murdered Indigenous Women and Girls. https://www.mmiwg-ffada.ca/video-clips/.

"K-W-L Chart." ReadWriteThink. International Literacy Association, NCTE. Downloadable PDF. http://www.readwritethink.org/classroom-resources/printouts/chart-a-30226.html.

L., A. "The Human Library Organisation Replaces Pages With People." *The Economist*, 3 November 2017. https://www.economist.com/prospero/2017/11/03/the-human-library-organisation-replaces-pages-with-people.

TEACHER GUIDE FOR SUGAR FALLS: A RESIDENTIAL SCHOOL STORY © 2021 PORTAGE & MAIN PRESS ISBN: 978-1-77492-010-7

Lackenbauer, P. Whitney, John Moses, R. Scott Sheffield, Maxime Gohier. "The Arrival of the Europeans: 17th Century Wars." *Aboriginal People in the Canadian Military*. Ottawa: Department of National Defense, 2018. https://www.canada.ca/en/department-national- defence/services/military-history/history-heritage/popular-books/aboriginal-people-canadian-military/arrival-europeans-17th-century-wars.html.

"A Lost Heritage: Canada's Residential Schools." CBC Digital Archives. CBC. https://www.cbc.ca/archives/topic/a-lost-heritage-canadas-residential-schools.

Manitoba Education and Youth. *Integrating Aboriginal Perspectives Into Curricula*. Government of Manitoba, 2003. https://www.edu.gov.mb.ca/k12/docs/policy/abpersp/ab_persp.pdf.

Manitoba First Nations Education Resource Centre Inc. https://mfnerc.org/resources/.

Provides resources and services to schools and hosts an amazing video library that showcases communities and culture.

Marshall, Tabitha, updated by David Joseph Gallant. "Indian Residential Schools Settlement Agreement." *Canadian Encyclopedia*, 16 January 2020. https://www.thecanadianencyclopedia.ca/en/article/indian-residential-schools-settlement-agreement.

Miller, Andrew. "Creating a Culture of Inquiry." *Edutopia* (blog), 8 September 2015. https://www.edutopia.org/blog/creating-a-culture-of-inquiry-andrew-miller.

Miller, James, updated by Zach Parrott. "Indigenous-British Relations Pre-Confederation." *Canadian Encyclopedia*, 26 May 2015. https://www.thecanadianencyclopedia.ca/en/article/aboriginal-european-relations.

Mosby, Ian. "The Legacy of Nutritional Experiments in Residential Schools." Moderated by Jo-Ann Archibald. Alumni UBC. Podcast, 1:46:13. 17 October 2014. https://www.alumni.ubc.ca/podcasts/the-legacy-of-nutritional-experiments-in-residential-schools/.

National Inquiry Into Missing and Murdered Indigenous Women and Girls. *Reclaiming Power and Place: The Final Report of the National Inquiry Into Missing and Murdered Indigenous Women and Girls*. Downloadable PDF in 2 vol. www.mmiwg-ffada.ca.

This website also has links to Key Moment Videos (https://www.mmiwg-ffada.ca/video-clips/) as well as information about the Truth Sharing Podcasts (https://www.mmiwg-ffada.ca/wp-content/uploads/2019/05/News-Release-The-Truth-Sharing-Podcasts-ENG.pdf).

"Ontario Natives Launch Residential School Lawsuit." *CBC News*, 20 June 2000. https://www.cbc.ca/news/canada/ontario-natives-launch-residential-school-lawsuit-1.240548.

"Residential Schools in Canada: History and Legacy Education Guide." Historica Canada Education Portal. http://www.education.historicacanada.ca/en/tools/647.

This page has links to two downloadable PDFs, the *Residential Schools in Canada: History and Legacy Education Guide* (Historica, 2016), and a set of accompanying worksheets.

"The Residential School System." Parks Canada. Government of Canada, 1 September 2020. https://www.canada.ca/en/parks-canada/news/2020/09/the-residential-school-system.html#shr-pg0.

"Resources and Downloads to Facilitate Inquiry-Based Learning." Edutopia. George Lucas Educational Foundation. 12 August 2016. https://www.edutopia.org/article/inquiry-based-learning-resources-downloads.

Resources for teachers that focus on the core strategies of comprehensive assessment, integrated studies, project-based learning, professional learning, social and emotional learning, and technology integration.

TEACHER GUIDE FOR SUGAR FALLS: A RESIDENTIAL SCHOOL STORY © 2021 PORTAGE & MAIN PRESS   ISBN: 978-1-77492-010-7

"Statement of Apology to Former Students of Indian Residential Schools." Crown-Indigenous Relations and Northern Affairs Canada. Government of Canada, 15 September 2010. https://www.rcaanc-cirnac.gc.ca/eng/1100100015644/1571589171655.

"The Story of Orange Shirt Day." Orange Shirt Society. https://www.orangeshirtday.org/about-us.html.

Truth and Reconciliation Commission of Canada. *Canada's Residential Schools: Reconciliation*. Vol. 6 of *The Final Report of the Truth and Reconciliation Commission of Canada*. Montreal: McGill-Queen's University Press, 2015. https://ehprnh2mwo3.exactdn.com/wp-content/uploads/2021/01/Volume_6_Reconciliation_English_Web.pdf.

———. *They Came for the Children: Canada, Aboriginal Peoples, and Residential Schools*. Winnipeg: Truth and Reconciliation Commission of Canada, 2012. http://publications.gc.ca/collections/collection_2012/cvrc-trcc/IR4-4-2012-eng.pdf.

TEACHER GUIDE FOR SUGAR FALLS: A RESIDENTIAL SCHOOL STORY © 2021 PORTAGE & MAIN PRESS ISBN: 978-1-77492-010-7

CHRISTINE M'LOT (she/her/hers) is an Anishinaabe educator and curriculum developer from Winnipeg, Manitoba. She has experience working with children and youth in multiple capacities including child welfare, children's disability services, and Indigenous family programming. She currently teaches high school at the University of Winnipeg Collegiate. Christine is also co-founder of Red Rising Education, and works to create Indigenous education resources for teachers.